From Far

CW00666474

To Getting There

Elizabeth Wright

First published in the UK in March 2013 by MyVoice Publishing

Published by: MyVoice Publishing,
Unit 1,
16 Maple Road,
Eastbourne,
BN23 6NY

ISBN: 978-1-909359-16-1

Elizabeth Wright

DEDICATED TO MY MUCH LOVED FAMILY

JACKIE and CHRIS

And grandchildren

BRIONY TYLER and JACK

From Fancy Pants to Getting There

Foreword

I spent several enthralled hours in coffee shops sniggering and chortling my way through this book ignoring the wary glances from other customers. Sometimes my rib cage was in pain from laughing so hard.

Life throws us many curved balls, both high and low, and Elizabeth's view on her life has a wit that allowed her to lift her head high and march on in the face of adversity. She saw silver linings around incidents ranging from a cheating husband, a short Italian bread waving shopkeeper, to a beloved daughter who keeps her focused.

Elizabeth's strode on through life dealing with divorce, dodgy accommodation with a Manager who hobbled around on an ill-fitting wooden leg, kitchen cockroaches and a pair of well filled trousers.

She had been running a pet store business for thirty eight years and then the recession hit; it slide down the tubes leaving her to face bankruptcy and a big mortgage. Her tales of various jobs from working in an Italian mob bakery to a flying bottle filling factory and observations of interesting people she met along the way, from a wheelchair drunk to terrorists, meant that Elizabeth was always looking with a different view on life.

It was in a dentist office that Elizabeth discovered the golden gem for writing and after a long hard haul one can say she's there – Humorist Author Extra-Ordinaire.

From a fellow Author and Poet

Audrey Chalifoux

From Fancy Pants to Getting There

From Fancy Pants to Getting There

The Discovery

Nearly knickers I would have called them; the open crotch winked brazenly at me from between his unwashed socks and empty fag packets that were stuffed into his overnight bag. With shaking hands I picked up this scrap of scarlet gossamer and gave it a closer look. Definitely not designed for comfort and, definitely not one of mine. I'd have been hard pressed to have got it halfway up my left leg. I felt sick as I visualised a pert, cellulite - free rear tucked inside the material. The words, "Till death us do part" were shortly going to have a new meaning when I caught up with him. His death - my part in it.

As usual, after long hours driving his lorry, he was enjoying his regular evening visit to the Pig and Whistle down the road, knocking back multiple pints of their strong local brew, having a few games of darts with his mates, and probably indulging in lecherous leers down the flirty landlady's walnut cracking cleavage.

Now that my suspicions of his cheating had been confirmed, I couldn't stop the tears of rage streaming down my face as I threw the offending piece of red material at the wall. "The bastard, I'll kill him, I will, I'll bloody kill him." A large spider, industriously weaving a web in the corner, suddenly found its delicate handiwork had been sliced in two by the descending underwear. It hastily retreated into a hole in the brickwork.

For a long time I had been aware that Tony, with his handsome, rugged looks, twinkly green eyes and quick wit, always turned on the charm when women were around. But, I didn't want to face the fact that he had often taken things further than just a social chat. As a fully paid up member of the 'Liars' Club' he always managed to cover his tracks and sweet talk his way out of trouble. Stupidly, I'd always wanted so much to believe him, hoping he'd change and settle down, especially as there was now Jackie, our beautiful baby girl in our lives, so I'd had a strong maternal urge to keep the family unit together. But, having turned a blind eye to his feckless womanising for twelve years, he was going to find out that thirteen would be his unlucky number.

Angrily rubbing the tears from my face, I finally had a light bulb moment and realised that I had to stop believing everything was going to be all right. Tony would never change.

I furiously zipped up his overnight bag, stood looking at this battered and stained bundle of mock leather and shouted, "Right, that's it, finish. End of the line." He had to go, one way or the other.

The First Date

It had all started out so well. He began working in a DIY shop two doors down from my pet shop. The attraction was instantaneous. I broke out in a hot flush from the moment he took off his shirt on a hot summer's day, revealing a bronzed, muscular body that I wanted to run my hands all over.

I was to find out that he was a manly man, one who sharpened his pencils with Stanley knives, knew exactly which screwdriver to use, "You need a posi for that job," and drinking the last two thirds of a pint of beer in one fluid movement before leaving the pub. He could nudge his car into the smallest of parking spaces and effortlessly undo stiff jam jar lids with a single twist, unaided by a hammer, chisel or bent tin opener.

Totally smitten, I pursued him unashamedly, turning a deaf ear to rumours of his serial philandering. My father, an ex-Metropolitan police officer, was far from happy. Using his detective skills, he turned up a lot about Tony's past love lives, where it appeared anything in a skirt was fair game. As a loving, caring father, he tried to warn me off, but at the age of twenty-eight, with my hormones exploding in all directions, I had fallen hopelessly in love for the first time. A love so overwhelming, nothing else mattered. "Dad," I said, "This is the man I want to set up home with, bear his children and grow old together in a loving relationship."

Dad obviously realised that the more he tried to put me off, the more I'd dig my heels in, so he simply looked pityingly at me and muttered, "I'm afraid you are going to find out in time, my girl, he's up to no good. A leopard never changed its spots."

All of this went over the top of my head as I ditched my dull wardrobe of ankle length dresses and boring cardigans in favour of short skirts, push up bras and high heeled fashion shoes that started to play havoc with my bunions. It didn't take Tony long to notice what was so obviously on offer and, and to my delight, he came into my shop shortly afterwards and, true to character, asked, "Would you like to come out for a drink tomorrow night?"

After work I rushed home, threw open my wardrobe door and frantically tried to find something suitable to wear, preferably eye - catching and blatantly sexy. But my updated outfits were definitely not right for this occasion. Visiting the stores in the shopping centre I came across a daringly short dress; in the changing room it looked great, but once I got home and had a test run in front of the mirror, I realised it was so revealingly short that bending over in company was not going to be an option.

The next evening I spent ages putting on more glamorous make – up and squirted plenty of 'special occasions only' Chanel No 5 all over my body. By adding silky tights and high heels I felt that I had scrubbed up quite well.

He turned up that evening in an immaculately polished, shiny red mini that sported a small brass aeroplane etched into the top of the gear stick. An acknowledgement to his RAF days. The vehicle's pristine perfection should have warned me that this man would always value his precious car above any relationship, however special. But, my marathon efforts at trying to look sexy were well worth the effort when he looked me over and said, "Wow, aren't you just gorgeous."

Excitedly, I got into his car and slammed the door. To my horror, the flimsy handle fell off and the door swung open.

I laughed nervously, "Sorry about that," I said, handing him the strip of metal. His face suddenly went from happy-smiley to bad-tempered bullfrog that's found something nasty at the bottom of the lily pond. He snatched a piece of string from the glove compartment, leaned over me and tied the door shut. He didn't utter a word and I was, at that point, tempted to bail out, but hesitated, as the possibilities of sex being on the menu added an emotional thrill to the situation.

Tony eventually thawed out when we found a traditional country pub and, sitting by a roaring fire gazing into each other's eyes, we mentally savoured what was likely to follow later. The back seat of that mini was going to take a pounding and he'd probably be seeing the soles of my feet in his wing mirror.

It was past midnight when we left, but, down a dark deserted country lane, the car engine started making peculiar noises and a cloud of steam gushed out from under the bonnet. Then the motor did a mechanical cough followed by a juddering hiccup, and died.

Tony's bad – tempered bullfrog face re-appeared. "Bloody thing," he muttered as he coasted the mini into a handy lay-by, parking alongside a dingy, brick building whose single, grubby 15 watt bulb barely illuminated a 'Public Conveniences' sign.

With the aid of a flickering torch, he angrily threw up the car bonnet and peered into the depths of the engine. After some pushing and poking, he emerged and said, "The water in the radiator needs topping up. Have a look in that 'Ladies' toilet and see if there's any taps or wash basins where we can get some water."

I gave my dress a downward hitch, undid the string on the door and went to investigate. In the 'Ladies,' the light inside was equally as dim as the one outside, but I could see a basin with a single, tarnished, cold water tap.

"Tony, there's water here but have you got a container I can fill up?"

"Nope. Use your imagination, woman, isn't there something in that building that we could use?"

A small metal dustbin stood invitingly nearby with a

very usable cover, although at that point, I was starting to feel annoyed by his grumpy attitude, and felt tempted to whack him on his head with it rather than carry water. But, not wanting to be stuck in the middle of the countryside with its rustlings and weird night noises, I took a deep breath and, juggling the lid between the basin and the tap, managed to persuade a small amount of water to trickle into it. Totterering on my four inch heels, I started to make my way back to the car. Then the torch expired and the light from the building's 15 watt bulb did little to illuminate the darkness.

"What the hell are you doing?"

"Can you put the headlights on so I can see where....." I slipped off the edge of the pavement, and, as I stumbled forward, the watery contents of the lid splattered over the exposed car engine.

"You stupid......" He switched on the headlights, grabbed a kitchen roll from the glove compartment and, ripping off yards of absorbent paper, tried to mop up the mess. He then vented his anger on the lid by snatching it out of my hands and hurling it away. It rolled across the road, doing noisy cartwheels along the tarmac.

"That was a stupid thing to do," I said, "Now how are we going to fill up the radiator?" No answer. I saw the lid had come to rest alongside the opposite pavement. So I retrieved it, kept my mouth shut and continued carrying water with greater care.

He eventually got the car going, but we had lost the little piece of string holding my door shut.

"Open your bloody window, stick your bloody arm out and hold that bloody door shut," he snarled at me. The frosty temperature inside was lower than the autumnal night outside. And the back seat wasn't even sat upon that night.

Family life

But, in spite of this hiccup, we continued to see one another and over a period of a year, the relationship blossomed. I decided to buy an old fashioned, roses-round -the - door cottage in the country. The roof had a couple of tiles missing, so when it rained water trickled down the bedroom wall; local field mice nipped in through a hole by the water pipe and scuttled noisily around the kitchen at night. We had to cope with a troublesome cesspit and all the cooking was done with bottled gas.

Tony said, "I'll do it all up and make it look nice," then hauled home great lengths of timber on his lorry and built himself a large garden shed, complete with an old portable TV fixed up high in one corner. He spent hours out there, watching football whilst planting seeds, potting up tomato plants, building fences for the garden and trellis for all the climbing roses.

But, I soon discovered that our choice of rural life was nowhere as idyllic as it was cracked up to be. As a night person, I was not the type to leap out of bed when the local rooster started his pre-dawn yodelling from the top of the hen house. After umpteen cock-a-doodles I felt like wringing his scrawny, iridescent green neck. Also I could have happily lived without the countryside pong of newly spread cattle slurry, considered by the locals as being 'a healthy smell'. I soon found out that where there are nasty niffs, there are flies. Hundreds of them, buzzing around, and some seemed to find something interesting in my kitchen. There they were, walking up and down my worktops with their dirty feet.

"This is not good," I said to Tony, "They've got germs."

So, he bought a zapper, screwed it to the wall and retreated to his garden shed. The apparatus sent out an inviting blue light, which proved to be brilliant at wasp disposal, they exploded on impact, but the incoming flies were not interested. I was forced to shut all the windows to keep them and the pong out. But the weather was reaching record breaking high temperatures so I had to open them again. Within minutes the flies were back. I carefully wiped down the kitchen work top surfaces with a mild solution of bleach, so they buzzed up to the ceiling and hung off the light fittings instead. Being environmentally friendly, I didn't want to start eliminating them with some lethal cocktail in a spray, but, alternatively, I didn't fancy hanging unsightly sticky fly papers around the room.

Then I saw some fly swats prominently displayed in the local DIY shop window, and thought, 'That's really eco-friendly, no chemical sprays,' I even had a choice of colours, red, green or blue. The handles were long and flexible, with a square of fine mesh at the top.

I gave one a 'test drive,' after all, I wasn't going to spend 75p if it didn't feel comfortable to use. Clutching the swat, I waved my arms around, hoping for an unexpected insect to appear, so I could then see how efficient this killing machine might be. Nothing obligingly buzzed by as I jumped around doing powerful Wimbledon style tennis serves, but this piece of plastic felt good in my hands and gave off a vicious twang as it swung through the air. I bought the blue one to match the colour scheme of my kitchen.

But any weapon is only as good as its user; I realised that I would need a robust approach to fly disposal, no squeamish cop-outs at the last moment. It had to be wham - bang, good bye fly. Little black bodies would have to be picked up off the floor with a tissue, or, I'd need to scrape bits of mashed fly from out the mesh. Stomach churning or not, my kitchen needed me. Tony just said, "You get on with it then," and retreated down to his garden shed.

Clutching my weapon of war, I advanced and whipped

it around in the general direction of a gang of flies circling around the strip light, hoping that after few good strikes some would be hit and brought down. But I discovered when you wave your arms around, you create air-waves which drive the flies away from you. A different approach was needed.

I studied their habits. There were various sizes and types of flies with differing airborne strategies. There were the ones that played 'chicken,' bombing in the window, whizz across the kitchen and zooming out the back door before I had time to grab the swat. The big, fat ones droned in sounding like mini lawn mowers, strutted their stuff, and then hung off the light fittings. The tiny ones played 'hide and seek,' doing a bit of camouflage and mingling with anything spotty. Other little flies simple flew crazily around in circles, as if high on speed rather than cow dung.

I soon learnt that it was near impossible to kill any in flight. A much better tactic was to wait until they had landed. I reckoned that when they were mentally engaged in downing their landing gear, I could use that split second to my advantage. But, the "Whoosh" of the swat coming down at ninety miles an hour, gave them enough warning to take avoiding action.

A successful kill had to come eventually, but at a price. A small fly, apparently snoozing on the strip light cover, gave me my perfect opportunity. Swat in hand, I approached cautiously and struck our recklessly. The dead fly fell to the floor, followed by the dented cover and the disintegrating four-foot tube.

I would need to switch to another, more efficient, method of fly disposal. I noticed that they dodged the swat when in flight and most escaped being whacked when walking on the work tops. They had to have a weak spot. With their brilliant eye-sight they could see me approaching from every direction and avoid sudden extermination. I realised that the only way I could score Brownie points was by meeting them head on as they took off.

My chosen quarry settled on the worktop, started to rub his hind legs together and give his face a bit of a wash. I slowly crept up, swat in hand, approaching from the front. He stopped his ablutions and stiffened in preparation to take off. I stood still. He relaxed and began licking his front leg with a stumpy tongue. I slowly raised the swat and, sensing danger, he crouched, taking up a 'ready – to - launch' position. For a brief moment he hesitated, then hurled himself upwards, to be met by my swat coming swiftly downwards. SPLAT!!

"Well, you sorted that one out," said Tony, watching from the doorway, "Now how about those other twenty or thirty on that lampshade?"

But flies were small fry compared to the next rustic life incident which occurred a few days after we'd moved in. I mistook the strangled screams from the adjacent woods as desperate cries from victims of a mass murder. With Tony away on a lengthy delivery for his company, I panicked and dialled 999. The local Bobbies, clearly longing for a bit of excitement on their quiet patch, arrived within minutes, blue lights flashing, and notebooks at the ready.

As they both strode up the garden path, I rushed out to meet them, hysterical at this apparently terrible situation.

"There's something dreadful going on up in those woods. I think someone is being killed. Listen, you can hear their screams."

From the depth of the velvet darkness came more loud moans and ear-splitting shrieks. I sobbed, "Can't you do anything, get more help? There's a murderer on the loose."

I had visions of dismembered bodies lying under oak trees; the odd severed hand or foot scattered amongst the blackberry bushes, and bloodied scalps hanging from branches.

But, as another wail reached our ears, they looked at one another and roared with laughter. I couldn't believe their indifference. People were dying just a short distance away and here they were laughing.

"What's the matter with you?" I was into a double dose of hysterics by now.

"How long have you lived here?" they asked. I sniffed. "Two days."

"That, my love, is the frustrated cry of a female fox looking for a bit of the other. It often happens at this time of the year."

He did seem a bit disappointed as he snapped his notebook shut, and, raising his eyes to heaven, turned back to the car, still laughing. I wondered what he had put in his book. Probably, 'Murder nil, fox 1. And watch out for that dopey female at 42 Harrods Farm Estate.'

Next time I heard suspicious noises from outside, I refrained from rushing to the phone. With Tony at home, we were sitting by an open window, enjoying the welcome coolness of a late summer's evening. From behind the hedge we heard loud rustling, snorting and sniffing. I nudged Tony as he was trying to extract hard bits of my toffee pudding from between his teeth.

"Listen to that," I said, "There's something funny going on out there."

He inspected the congealed blob stuck firmly in his fingernail. I nudged him again as the eerie noises continued, now accompanied by heavy breathing.

"What is it?" I whispered, the hairs on the back of my neck prickling.

"I don't know," replied Tony, "But we'll soon find out."

He dragged open the drawer by the sink and from amongst the spare plugs, hot water bottle, mouse traps and assorted rubbish, he found a heavy spanner, and a rusty torch that appeared to be a just case for dead batteries. But after thumping it on the worktop a few times, a glimmer of light appeared.

We eased open the front door and cautiously looked out. The noises stopped. We stood still and held our breath, straining to see into the darkness. The branches of a nearby fuchsia bush jiggled violently as something brushed by it. The snuffling started again, and by the fading light from the torch we saw a small dark ball moving through the grass. A black dribbly nose wiggled in the air.

"It's a hedgehog," I laughed with relief, and without thinking, scooped it up. "Isn't it adorable?" I promptly learnt that hedgehogs don't like being handled or stroked; this one immediately curled its prickly body tightly, and painfully, around my fingers and a multitude of fleas emerged from its spines, jumped onto my arm and started to bite me.

"That was a silly thing to do," commented Tony as he tore off strips of sticking plaster to cover the bleeding holes in my hand, at the same time trying to flick off feeding fleas.

Once we'd got settled in and sorted out our new home, we started exploring the surrounding countryside, and came across the remains of a disused railway track hidden away in the folds of a meadow. Under brilliant blue skies we both felt at one with nature, the world was a million miles away. Skylarks were singing overhead, swallows wheeling in the sky. Bees were hovering in the buttercups, the long grasses whispered in the gentle breeze…this was romantic heaven.

We gazed into each other's eyes. "I love you," he said, and gently undid my dress so it slipped down to my ankles. I lovingly, but lustily, ripped his clothes off and our naked bodies came together in a passionate embrace as we slowly descended onto a bed of soft green grass.

The bees droned on around us, oblivious to our ecstasy, all, that was, except one. She had been quietly gathering her nectar from a flower, not bothering anyone, when this big, pink bottom suddenly flattened her little world. She then did what all bees do in stressful situations, she put her sting into operation, right into the offending posterior. Tony leapt up, viciously stamped on the stunned insect, and shouted a few choice swear words that made the sheep run away in the adjacent field.

Passion dispelled, we put our clothes back on. I did offer to try and tease the sting out from the now reddening patch on his rump, but was told to "f*** off" as he carefully eased his trousers up. Trying to make light of the situation, I flirtingly said, "Never mind, there's always another time to have fun in the sun." I rumpled his hair, kissed his forehead, ran my hand up his now clothed leg, grabbed his trouser zip and yanked it swiftly up to the waistband....the hospital said, 'Yes, they had had previous experience of disengaging zips from delicate parts of male anatomies, and did he want the bee sting sorted out at the same time?'

Sid, a friend of Tony's found the incident highly amusing, and dabbling a bit in poetry, he gave Tony a slip of paper ....

'Tony when young, was romantic,
And thought that courting was fine.
He and his lady love would go roaming
Down alongside the old railway line.

They knew the times the trains went by
They knew them off by heart,
For courting is a serious play,
And Tony loved the part.

One warm and sunny afternoon
It's really not surprising,

As they walked their favourite haunt
They found their passions rising.

Gently he held her in his embrace,
As softly to the ground they fell,
But before he had even kissed her
He let out one hell of a yell.

The place they had chosen was secluded,
Under one old crab apple tree,
And the cause of all his commotion
He had gone and sat on a bee.

Now Liz his lover, was a practical girl,
And offered to render first aid.
But Tony, with blushes, declined saying
I've never yet shown my **** to a maid.

Now the moral of this story is
Don't court by the line under trees.
The couch in the parlour is perfect,
Where you can do it with ease, without bees.

Baby Time

Some weeks later, when Tony was perched precariously up on the top of the tall steps pruning a rampant yellow climbing rose, I found out that I had some unexpected and exciting news to tell him. There was a blue line on the pregnancy testing kit. I rushed outside and, holding up the little plastic stick, I said, "Tony, Tony, I've something wonderful to tell you."

Clip, clip. "Oh, yes, what?" Clip, clip.

A few green branches fell at my feet. There was a delicate smell of crushed rose petals in the air.

"You're going to be a dad."

Clip, clip. More cuttings tumbled down.

He paused.

"What did you say?" I waved the stick in the air, "You're going to be a dad, its positive."

Clip, clip. CLIP.

The climbing rose suddenly became a traumatised floribunda, as a large section of mutilated blossom tumbled to the ground, followed by the collapsing steps and a visibly shocked Tony.

I rushed forward to check he was all right. He sat up, vigorously rubbed his bruised bottom and scratched arms and said, "No, no, no, that can't be right, are you absolutely sure?"

"Well, these testing kits are pretty accurate."

"But you're pushing forty - three, I'm fifty – five, we don't have babies at our age."

"Well, it looks as if we are."

After puffing on a few cigarettes held with shaking hands, followed by a couple of stiff drinks, he decided that he quite liked the idea of being a dad. It seemed that there could be some kudos to be earned when he told his mates down the pub.

A few days later he came home after work and pressed a small box into my hands.

"What's this?"

"Open it and you'll see."

Inside was an eternity ring, a circle of red and white stones.

"Put it on. This is to say thank you for making me a dad." He kissed me on the cheek.

"Tomorrow you go down to the doctor's surgery and get yourself checked out." He settled himself in the armchair and turned the TV on.

I twirled the gift around my finger. "Tony, this is beautiful."

"That's all right then; now get me a cup of tea."

The romantic gesture was short lived, before I had dished up his dinner he'd fallen asleep. I looked at him, still sat up, his head lolling on one side and a dribble of saliva trickling down the side of his chin. Where would life take us from here?

Pregnancy, Hospitals And New Baby

"Now, you've got to take life easy, remember your age," said my doctor, after twanging his rubber gloves in preparation for an exploratory search into my nether regions. I didn't dare tell him that, prior to my visit, and the day before the test result, I had helped a delivery driver to shift a tonne of grain from off his lorry into my pet shop storeroom.

After some pushing, prodding and poking the doctor emerged, peeled off the gloves and said, "You're about three months gone and I think you've got twins in there." Two babies! As wrinklies Tony and I were probably equally ill-equipped to cope with even one baby. How was I going to tell him that our future offspring had just multiplied?

I approached him cautiously when he arrived home. "I've got some news for you." I passed him a big mug of tea hoping this might smooth the way.

"What?"

Tricky this. I took a deep breath. "You are going to be a dad to twins."

His hands started to shake. He fished around in his pockets for the inevitable packet of cigarettes. Having lit one, he noisily took a few puffs whilst giving gave the situation some thought. Another time I was going to have to tell him that in the future smoking cigarettes in the home was bad for the babies.

He banged the cup down and hot tea slopped onto the table.

"I'm going out."

He put on his coat, took himself off to the pub, and returned late, blind drunk. The sofa was his preferred choice to crash out on, so I went to bed, leaving him with his head hung over the edge of the cushions, a bucket

17

strategically placed underneath.

In a short space of time he mellowed slightly, and brought home assorted toys and baby clothes. On returning from one delivery trip he opened the back doors of his van and carefully pulled out a classy double buggy.

"That's absolutely lovely," I said, "I bet that was expensive, I ought to give you something towards the cost."

He looked at me and winked.

"Fell off the back of a lorry."

No more was said.

As the weeks went by my expanding body was no longer my own. Pregnancy had brought with it morning sickness that got me throwing up around bedtime, my gums got soft and my sense of smell went. I ate pickled onions by the dozen because they were the only food that I could taste. Everything else seemed to have the texture and flavour of flaky cardboard.

Because of my age, it was often suggested at hospital visits that I would need extra care during this pregnancy.

"Don't you think you should have known better at your age," said one white coated doctor, staring intently at my notes.

Feeling annoyed I retorted, "Well, doc, I've been trying for twelve years and I've finally got a result, well two, actually."

He ignored this and sent me to one of the hospital nurses for a blood test. Those two words sent a shiver down my spine. Anything to do with needles being jabbed into any part of my anatomy and I'm gone. But I'd got two little ones to think of now, love, care and common sense over ruled the urge to leg it. By the time my name was called, I'd talked myself into some state of calmness.

"My, you have got lovely veins, you should be a blood donor," enthused Dracula's daughter, binding my arm and jabbing the needle into an obliging vein that had popped up. It seemed ages before the phial was filled with dark red liquid.

"There you are, all done," She whipped out the needle, slapped a tiny piece of sticking plaster over the hole and told me to press my fingers down gently on top of it.

"To stop the bruising," she explained. I just wanted my blood back before I passed out on the floor.

"See you in a few weeks."

When I went for the scan, we could all see there was only one baby. Had there ever been two? We would never know. We called a halt to buying two of everything, and traded the double buggy for a single one. Because of my age, forty-two, it was suggested that an amniocentesis test could be carried out to detect Downs Syndrome.

This involved using a long needle stuck into my stomach to extract fluid from the placenta. Testing would then tell if there were any abnormalities. The downside was that before the appointed time I was asked to drink a quantity of water.

On the day of the examination, having filled up with fluid, I wrapped the piece of blue checked material that passed as a hospital gown around my naked body, and entered the room to meet the team of nurses and obstetrician. Smiling and cheerful, they carefully laid me on the operating table, and put up a small green screen across my waist so I couldn't see what they were doing.

"Now," said one of the men in white coats, "We're just going to give you a local anaesthetic in your stomach, just a tiny prick, no more than a bee sting." Four jabs later and I finally declared I couldn't feel anything in my stomach area. I just hoped my bladder was still under control.

"Now, we're just going to draw off some fluid around the placenta for testing." Mr. White Coat made the mistake of holding up the needle a bit too high. I could see it over the top of the little screen. Had he picked the wrong implement from his tool box, as this one looked like a lengthy drill bit used for making holes in thick brick walls?

"Now, I'm just going to put the needle in gently."

It felt as if an elephant had sat on my numb stomach as he forced this instrument of torture into my distended tissue. As he did so, wind in my stomach suddenly found an alternative exit and exploded past the needle as a loud, lengthy fart. I had the urge to pull my knees together to stop the contents of my over full bladder from following suit.

After a great deal of probing, pushing and consultation, the crew decided that because the baby was in the wrong position, they couldn't draw off the necessary liquid. So, I was sent home with a bit of sticky dressing over the red patch on my stomach and told I'd have to go through it all again in four weeks.

This time they were successful and after testing the fluid I received a phone call. All was well, and did I want to know the baby's sex?

"Oh, yes."

"You're having a little girl."

A daughter. I could see her in pretty dresses with curly hair. She'd probably be a daddy's girl, but we could have girly chats as she grew.

"We're having a little girl," I told Tony. He'd mellowed a lot and was delighted at the news; he came home with more armfuls of cuddly toys and a book of children's names. Choosing one was difficult, we each had differing ideas, but when we reached the 'J's' and saw Jacqueline,

"I like that," said Tony, "What do you think?"

"Yes, I like that name too."

During the hospital visits for routine check-ups, clutching the obligatory filled sample bottle, there wasn't a nook or cranny of my body that someone hadn't looked up or into, probed and injected. As a teaching hospital, trainees sat in on most of my examinations. I was taking my clothes off so often that I seriously began to think that after the birth I could add to my income by becoming a stripper, especially as my boobs had inflated to granite filled balloons. This was brought to the attention of the young would-be doctors and midwives. A nurse took me aside and asked, "As you are an older mum, would you mind if one or two of our students here have a feel of your breasts so they get an idea of how they can change in pregnancy?"

As I took off my blouse and bra the nearest young man appeared not to know where to look.

"It's all right, I really don't mind, go ahead." Being pregnant, my readjusted hormones had made me exceptionally easy going.

He stood in front of me, both hands held up, cupped, as if he was ready to catch a couple of balls. His face had gone bright red, and there were beads of sweat on his upper lip. After further persuasion from me he gave my flesh a few tentative squeezes and retreated. In spite of his awkwardness, I concluded that his experience of fondling a patient's boobs, and being paid for it, was going to be a good talking point in the students' bar that night.

Delivery date should have been the 1st June, but it was decided two weeks earlier that an induction would be the preferred method. The doctor said, "There's no point in leaving the baby in there any longer."

Having packed my bag I went to hospital the night before for a check over. On delivery day I settled cosily into a comfortable bed in preparation for the delivery. I winced as a 3-way cannula was put into a vein in my hand, administering medication to get the show on the road. This was at 11am. Nothing happened. The doses were upped. Still nothing happened. No contractions. I was so cosy I had a snooze. Then I fancied some fish and chips.

"Any movement yet?"

"Not yet."

Tony turned up after work, but was so drunk he was diplomatically escorted out. I was on my own.

At 4pm I was shaken out of my lethargy by two hefty contractions and we were away. Fast. I was hitched up to a copy of Cape Canaveral's launching pad, and everyone was having a good look up my insides to see if Jackie was on her way out. To distract myself from the cramping pains I started counting the red painted tulips decorating one wall. Just as I was about ready to push, it all stopped. Jackie had got stuck.

Out came a pair of what looked like large sugar tongs, and efforts were made to pull her out by grabbing onto her head. All that the forceps got hold of was a bunch of thick black hair. Jackie, it seemed, had decided to stay put.

Plan B meant intervention with the help of a scalpel, cutting me open to get her out. Jackie slithered into the world at 9.25pm and gave a gentle cry. Whilst she was being cleaned and checked over, I was having my sliced bits and pieces stitched back together. It took so long to patch me up that I thought the nurse was doing some running repairs on the hem of her uniform at the same time. Bruised and battered, I accepted that I would be eating my meals off the mantelpiece for the next week or so.

Even afterwards, as I lay in bed back in the ward, looking at this plastic cot containing the most beautiful baby in the world, somebody wanted more of my blood. After extracting and testing yet another phial full, the nurse came back and gave me a strange look.

"Do you feel all right?" she enquired. "Yes, I feel fine," I replied. "Well, according to this test, your blood count is so low, you should be a body in that bed. We'll need to give you a transfusion." As I'd gone right off needles, I declined, and chose instead, a course of iron tablets. Bad choice, I had to put up with running jokes about passing bricks as the slow moving contents of my intestines turned rock hard. But my other aperture freely relinquished all the cotton that had been used to stitch me up. As I sat in the hospital bath each day, with salt shaken in to help the healing, bits of dissolving green surgical string made their escape and floated to the surface.

When we went home, Tony proudly took his new daughter out to show all his friends. When I wheeled her out for the first time, a passer-by asked, "What's it like being a granny then?"

With a baby in our midst, our home routine altered. Tony was away most days driving a van delivering flower seed trays to much of southern England's garden centres. I went back to work in the pet shop, Jackie was in her pram in the back room, where I could watch her from the shop. My relationship with Tony started to slip away. We were both constantly tired, and, on opening a packet of contraceptive pills, I thought, "There's not much point in taking these." Sex had become just a word, no longer an action.

Out shopping, having bought more nappies, formula milk and bibs, I saw a nightie hung on a store rail. Not any old nightie, this was seductively diaphanous with tiny shoulder straps and plunging neckline. And breathtakingly expensive. I took it off the rail and held it up. After all, it wasn't going to cost anything to have a closer look. It was beautiful, just the thing to spice up our love life. I studied the price ticket.

'Go on,' a little voice said in my head, 'the business can afford it, and you should treat yourself occasionally.' But how could I justify that sort of price just for some nightwear. I put it back and walked away.

But its image followed me, haunted me. As I pushed

the pram, everything I looked at was covered with this blue gossamer nightie trimmed with white lace. I visualised myself whirling and dancing like Ginger Rogers, the material flowing and rippling around my body. But I couldn't spend that sort of money. But the nightie beckoned. I had another look at the price ticket. It was too much. 'No it isn't,' said the little voice in my head. 'If it makes the two of us happy, then it is money well spent. Right, I'll buy it.'

I took the nightie off the rail, and, glowing with pleasure held it up again. This time there was no doubt in my mind. At the cash desk I laid it carefully across the counter and stood back admiring it, hopeful in my expectations of nights of endless love.

I couldn't wait to get home to try it on. Once in the front door, Jackie was placed in her cot for her afternoon sleep, the shopping bags were thrown onto the kitchen table and I hurried upstairs with the carrier containing my blue nightie. Even without a body inside, it promised sex and seduction. Once on, it curved and clung just where it should, teasingly revealing my body beneath.

Ah, the body, still a bit rough from childbirth; to live up to the nightie, that meant a detailed overhaul. Before Tony came home, I'd washed my hair, shaved my legs, cleaned my teeth, painted my fingernails a delicate shade of pale pink and carefully applied my makeup.

The front door slammed. Head in curlers, wrapped in a dressing – gown, I gave Tony a hug and asked, "Had a good day, darling?" He grunted, patted the top of Jackie's head and gave me a peck on the cheek, deftly removing the mug of tea from my hand. Another grunt as he lowered his frame onto the settee and pointed the remote at the television. The early evening news came on, wars and politics and how a swan had stopped all the traffic on the M25. I lovingly put his meal tray on his lap, and gave him the sort of smile that tried to say, 'Have I got a surprise for you later on!' He gave me a puzzled look whilst shovelling baked potato and beans into his mouth.

I went upstairs and slowly slipped into the nightie. It whispered and rustled as it slid down my body. I put a touch of perfume on my wrists, behind my ears and down my lace enfolded cleavage. Having brushed my hair, I looked in the mirror and thought, 'Pretty good.' This was going to be some night.

From the fridge in the kitchen I withdrew a bottle of chilled white wine, and hoping to catch Tony's attention, draped myself seductively against the lounge doorpost. In keeping with the mood of the occasion, I murmured in what I hoped was a husky, but sexy voice, "Hello gorgeous." He didn't look up; the only response I got was a grunt. He was far more interested in the loud shouts and cheering that were coming from the television. Determined not to take second place to whatever he was watching, I decided a live floor show could beat that. I slid in front of the screen and adopted a Mae West stance, one hand behind the back of my head, hips swaying, and motor running. "Come and get me," I purred, sliding one delicate strap off my shoulder. He looked up, face flushed, eyes bright. Definitely excited. He leaned forward, his arms reaching out towards me. I waited in eager anticipation for his hands to caress the responsive curves beneath the blue material, to gently tease the nightie from my body……

He touched me and then tried to move me to one side. I got ready for us to plunge onto the settee for a passionate sexy session. His voice uttered words of deep emotion, "Move over woman, can't you see Arsenal's just about to score."

The relationship finally went into freefall when I had to face the fact that I had serious competition in the bedroom department. Little signs, like the condoms hidden in the lining of his overnight bag, a vague smell of a strange perfume on his clothes, lack of interest in home life and then finding another woman's underwear in his bag. Local gossip confirmed all of my suspicions. So, after twelve years together, his persistent womanising finally drove me to the edge. I'd had enough. Murder was what I had in mind.

Revenge And The Parting

In a blind rage, I rummaged through the cutlery drawer, searching for the biggest and nastiest knife that I could find. I pounced on one with a deliciously pointed end that gleamed wickedly under the light. Waving it about I wondered whether six inches of best Sheffield steel would work more efficiently if I stabbed, or chopped, into his now rotund, double-crossing, sixteen stone frame.

Alternatively, there was a good solid axe in the garden shed. It lay just inside the door, a thick wedge of metal attached to a stubby wooden handle. Honed to perfection for cutting firewood, the silver edge of the blade would go through his flabby flesh like a knife through butter. I could even chop his lying, cheating head off with that.

Holding the axe in one hand and the knife in the other, I weighed up my options as to the best method of disposal. Either way, there was going to be a lot of blood and gore. Then I hesitated and took a realistic look at the situation. It would take weeks to get the kitchen clean again, how could I get rid of the body and I felt faint at the sight of blood. Murder gets you put in prison. Who would look after baby Jackie whilst I was doing time? The alternative? Give him his marching orders, let miss fancy pants do all his dirty washing, put up with his musical farts and clean off the thick tide marks he'd leave after he'd had a bath. And let her worry about where he would try and get his leg over next. Revenge is a dish best served cold, they say. After two deep, calming breaths, my well-filled platter was now on its way to join the icebergs in the Arctic Ocean.

I picked Jackie up from her cot and nipped next door to my best friend Sadie, because I really needed someone to talk to. She had a heart as big as a house and was constantly "rescuing" people or pets. Her home was filled with unwanted creatures, elderly dogs, one legged cats and black rats. In the corner of the front room was a huge aquarium housing a slithery collection of chunky land snails. In the garden she had rows of cages full of dumped doe rabbits that turned out a steady flow of grey babies without the apparent essential input of a male rabbit. "Virgin births or divine intervention" was Sadie's absolute belief in this peculiar phenomenon. But her faith in the miraculous or magical was shattered when she discovered a randy male wild rabbit was regularly nipping through a well-dug hole under her garden fence and enthusiastically, if somewhat awkwardly, servicing rows of 'come and get us' bottoms pressed eagerly up against the hutch wires.

Two of her many cats were noisily copulating on the cracked concrete pathway, watched by three others sitting on the roof of her old green CV with its "Witches do it in circles" stuck crookedly across the back window. I knocked on her door and a chunk of peeling red paint fell off.

Sadie dragged open the door. Year of decay and assaults by inclement weather had rendered it almost inoperable. She took one look at my tear-stained, stony face and sleepy baby in my arms and asked, "Oh Liz, what's wrong?"

"Look," - I thrust the red material up to her face. "See this, I found it in his overnight bag, he's obviously having it off with someone else."

She inspected the thong.

"Could be a present for you."

"Don't be daft; even he couldn't mix up buying a size zero when I'm a size sixteen. That's a conquest souvenir."

Sadie, ever the peacemaker, started trying to be helpful.

"Come and sit down, have a cup of tea and get it off your chest, love." But what I'd started I was going to finish.

"Can you do me a favour and baby - sit Jackie for a while. I've got things to do. He's gone down the pub."

"You're not going to do anything silly, are you?" she asked, taking Jackie from my arms. I stuffed the knickers into my pocket.

"Nope."

Oblivious to the cold February wind, I stormed off down the road to the Pig and Whistle. Various methods of confrontation went through my mind. Should I open the pub door, wave the red knickers in the air, yelling, "Which hussy did you get these off then?" Or jam them on his head in the crowded bar and then walk out, leaving him to do the explaining. By the time I got there I was beginning to frighten myself with some of the wicked things I wished I could do to him, castration with a pair of garden shears being one of the kinder options.

His car was in the car park. A new, bright red Capri, long, low and loud, a typical choice for a middle aged man with something to prove. He always drove it with the window open, radio on full blast, hand out the window clutching the inevitable fag, dark glasses on, completing an image that could have been ruined by the sight of a baby seat in the back. Knowing this car was his pride and joy made me feel spiteful enough to want to smash it to bits. It shimmered under the pub lights, waxed and lovingly polished. Not a mark on it. Then I knew exactly what I was going to do. I pulled out the knickers, threw them down, and with my heel, ground them into the gritty, oily sludge of the car park. When they were gratifying soiled, I used them to liberally smear muddy slime all over the spotless bodywork until it was scratched and filthy. With a final flourish, I tied a big knot in the top of the car aerial and spiked the dripping remnants of the Anne Summers flimsies on the top. I stood back, and with adrenaline still pounding through my body, looked at my handiwork with vitriolic pleasure. He would absolutely hate that.

The pub door suddenly opened and a laughing crowd spilled out - amongst them I spotted Tony. He was well tanked up and leaning slightly to starboard, the usual fag stuck in the corner of his mouth. He looked in horror at the revolting state of his Capri, his gaze travelling upwards to the tattered frillies fluttering in the breeze. Then he saw me and tried to pull himself together. I pointed to the knickers.

"You bloody bastard. What were those doing in your bag? Who's been getting their knickers off and their knockers out for you this time?"

The end of his cigarette glowed bright red as he took a couple of nervous puffs. Opting for the coward's way out, he retreated to the car and tried to get the key in the lock. Drink made that difficult.

I was not going to let him get away so easily. He'd trashed my life, and Jackie's. Bottled up emotions began to spill out as I tried to hit him around his head. I missed as he finally got the door open and attempted to scramble in; I snatched it out of his hands. The growing crowd were sniggering and lapping it all up. Tony struggled to get the door pulled shut, but I refused to let it go. My trump card was following.

"I've fucking had enough of you and all your womanising, your hollow promises and cheating ways. I'm sick of it all, we'll be better off without you. You can pack your bags and go and live with miss fancy pants. We're finished."

His face turned purple as he spluttered, "You bloody bitch." He wrenched the door from my grasp. I grabbed it back. It started going to and fro like the proverbial fiddler's elbow before he finally banged it shut, hastily started the engine and tried to find first gear. Nasty crunching noises emanated from the gear box as he revved up, and instead of moving forwards, the car shot backwards and smashed into a pansy filled wooden flower box, lovingly crafted out of half an old beer barrel. Its broken metal band hooked itself onto his bumper, and, with mini garden centre in tow, he careered onto the main road and was picked up by a prowling police car as he drove erratically home, carving muddy furrows into lengths of the grass verges.

As I walked past, smugly pleased that for once there was a policeman about when you wanted one, I heard him being asked, as he vainly tried to blow into the little bag to measure his alcohol levels, "What were you trying to do sir, plant up the A272?" He eventually came home, ignored me, went into the bedroom and slammed the door. I was past caring.

In the following days, when we both came home from work, I cooked meals just for myself, only did my own laundry, fussed over Jackie and slept in the other bedroom. He spent most evenings getting drunk down the pub and made no apparent effort to move out.

After about a week I dropped a hefty hint by putting all his stuff into black bin bags and throwing them down the garden path. Around midnight, as I sat in bed reading a book, I heard the front door crash open. He staggered into the bedroom and looked at me with hate in his eyes. Jackie whimpered in her sleep.

"You bloody horrible bitch," he shouted, and, in an alcohol-fuelled rage,

grabbed my arm, dragged me out of bed and hauled me along the corridor to the lounge. I screamed and tried to struggle free, but he was far too strong. His big, powerful hands went around my neck; he pushed me up against the wall, banging my head against the brickwork. I couldn't breathe. Jackie started to cry at the commotion. As I desperately tried to fight him off, I spotted an old wooden clock on the nearby mantelpiece.

I made a grab for it, and, with the last bit of strength that I could muster, hit him hard on the side of his head with this solid 1920's style reproduction. He staggered back, a look of amazement on his face, and stood watching as I desperately tried to breathe in. When air eventually hit my collapsing lungs, I couldn't stop coughing and choking. Then I was sick. He mumbled something, flopped down onto the settee and passed out.

Being bloody – minded enough not to run away, but fearful he might get drunk and have another try at eliminating me, I decided that the generous sized kitchen knife might, after all, come in useful as means of defence. Having got it from the drawer, I put it under my pillow, locked the bedroom door, and soothed Jackie back to sleep.

In the morning I cautiously peered around the lounge door and was relieved to find that Tony had already gone to work, leaving just crumpled cushions on the sofa. He didn't return that evening. The next day when Jackie and I came home, he'd departed, taking everything he owned with him. Only hangers were left in the empty wardrobe and all his tools had gone from his garden shed. There was nothing to show that he had ever lived here. Strangely, the little home felt empty without his presence. Jackie didn't seem bothered that her daddy wasn't around.

After having a good cry I decided to stop feeling sorry for myself, draw a line under the relationship and start afresh. That bitterly cold February, with challenging snowdrifts piled across the country lane, finally made up my mind for me. I thought, 'I've had enough of this. I'm moving. Commuting miles to work down country lanes, playing Russian roulette with snow filled ditches, scraping ice off the car each winter's morning, praying it would start, then coming home and trying to light a fire, where the twigs and kindling always seemed damp and the lumps of coal emitted foul-smelling smoke and took an age to give out any cosy heat.'

Someone new could get all excited about the misplaced charms of the countryside. I'd be moving into town with street lighting, shops around the corner, central heating and where boots with persistent strange odours were no longer essential footwear.

Before I had really realised it, the estate agent had sent me six prospective buyers who were all eager to buy my rural retreat, and within a short time I had a generous cheque in the bank but no new home to move into.

New Moves With Sex Thrown In

"I'm not moving that far away, probably only about ten miles down the road," I told Sadie. "We'll still easily be able to keep in touch. Jackie and I are moving into temporary accommodation near my business whilst we house hunt."

Having packed up everything we didn't need and put it into store, we booked into "The Festival," a rambling, Victorian building containing a collection of rooms spread over three shops, all of which had seen better days. Our third floor accommodation consisted of a generous lounge overlooking a main road with a little bedroom tucked behind. On each floor the toilets and bathrooms were shared.

Vera and Doug owned the property. Vera was a bleached blonde of mature years, who was overgenerous with the bright red lipstick. Her substantial bust was encased in tight white blouses through which you could see the top bits of her Alston's corsets, and her skirts of varying colours were a bit too tight and a bit too short.

Doug was a dour Scotsman, some twenty years older, who only had one leg. He used a wooden artificial limb, but it fitted him badly, so he swayed about when in forward motion, rather like a ship on stormy seas. Without his two walking sticks for extra support he occasionally stumbled or fell over, and the false leg used to detach itself from his lower half and drop with a bang out of the bottom of his trousers. This happened quite frequently when he was getting out of his car. The false leg would plonk noisily into the gutter, much to the consternation of passers-by. The less said the better, as to how he went about re-attaching it.

The other inhabitants were a transient mixture of students, couples on housing lists and elderly, long-term residents. We all had access to our accommodation either through the glass door at the rear of the downstairs restaurant, which Doug owned, or there was the dreaded 'back entrance.' This was the one that Vera preferred we use, as going through the eatery, trailing kids, prams and clutching bundles of supermarket shopping bags, in her opinion, 'gave the place a downbeat reputation.'

The back entrance was reached by a scruffy alleyway filled with rubbish and abandoned trolleys. You then had to go through a wide gate leaning at a drunken angle, into a jungle of a back garden and up a black fire escape. Through years of neglect, some of its fixings had parted company from the wall and the whole structure wobbled violently every time anyone went up or down the steps.

At the top was the communal kitchen. Everyone shared the plates, cutlery and cooking utensils and was expected to do their own washing up afterwards. With the usual spirit of co-operation no one bothered much with that. The food-encrusted pots could have pushed germ warfare into the next century. In the grill-pan you couldn't tell where the incinerated food ended and the metal began. Under these circumstances, oven-ready meals proved popular. Unwrap, bung them in, and throw the containers away afterwards. Simple. Only nobody made any attempt to empty the overflowing bin either.

Once a week, Sheila came in to do a bit of cleaning in Vera and Doug's rooms and she would pass a mop over the sticky kitchen floor, and occasionally take pity on the mounds of dirty crockery. Doug would make periodic visits to the kitchen and blow his top at the general mess, and for a few days, things would improve. But the room had a dingy, grubby appearance, smelt of cooking fat and brown Windsor soup, and the faded lino on the floor was crumbling into little bits. The old pine table in the centre of the room was covered in dubious stains, cigarette burn craters and galloping bacteria.

Coming in from the pictures late one night, I groped my way up the fire escape and unlocked the back door. The kitchen was in darkness. Someone had, for once, decided to comply with the notice, which said, "Please turn off the lights." Just as I started to walk through and collect Jackie from one of the students who had obligingly baby sat, I heard a strange tapping on the lino. In the half light from an emerging moon, the floor appeared to be moving. Flicking on the light switch, the single 40w bulb illuminated an army of cockroaches running scared in every direction. I screamed and began jumping on them to try and squash as many as I could. But cockroaches are made of tough stuff. Squashed, or minus limbs, they keep on going. I grabbed a huge carving knife from one of the drawers and hacked away at the dark bodies. Even divided in two they still moved. Hysterical, I jumped and stabbed until all the visible bits were still. Hundreds had escaped under the cupboards and cooker.

As I stood there, trembling, with the carving knife at the ready in case a single bold insect dared show its face, a voice from the inner door enquired, "What on earth are you doing?" I looked up and promptly fell in love with lust, gawping at this handsome stranger with sleek, shiny black hair, smooth suntanned skin and liquid brown 'come to bed' eyes. And as least twenty years younger than me.

"I'm killing cockroaches," was the only thing I could think of to say. He laughed, showing tidy, white teeth and my heart began leaping around so much I thought it would start knocking the buttons off the front of my dress.

"Oh well, that's all right then, I thought you had come to murder somebody. By the way, I moved in today, my name's Everard." I glanced down at his well-filled trousers and thought, "Yes, you probably are." But I smiled politely and said, "I'm Liz, I'm here for a while with my little daughter Jackie whilst we are house hunting."

The resultant handshake was electric, and comatose bits of my body perked up. Being celibate since Tony's departure, I suddenly realised what a lot I'd been missing.

We met the next day as we both pushed our foil-encased dinners into the oven together. As the meals cooked, symbolically side-by-side, he told me he was learning to be a mechanic and, when he got his qualifications he was off to Australia. Like a silly love-struck schoolgirl I sat with my chin cupped in my hands and drooled, never noticing Jackie was pouring cherryade into her shoe. As he told me all about his hopes and dreams, I discovered I wasn't that bothered about my future, I just wanted to get my sex starved body coupled with his. But good breeding prevented me from being so forward, although my body chemistry didn't give a hoot. He only had to look at me and I went all unnecessary. "Come in sometime for a drink," he invited, and I flushed. We both knew exactly what the score was, but I didn't want to be regarded as easy. After all, I was old enough to be his mother. I began to wonder if he needed glasses.

"Give it time," I murmured, relishing the thought that I'd have his trousers off by tomorrow.

But, at nine that night, just as I was reading yet another bedtime story to Jackie, trying to get her off to sleep in the little bedroom, there was a knock on the door. There in a short, silk dressing gown, stood Everard, living up to his name. I couldn't help thinking, 'If he doesn't watch out he might be in need of permission from local government planning regulations for that more or less permanent erection.'

He held a bottle of wine and two glasses.

"Look darling," I said to Jackie, trying to disguise my excitement, "Here's uncle Everard with a present for mummy." She glared at him from beneath her duvet. The 'go and get lost' look only a jealous three year old can give.

Everard draped himself comfortably into the big settee and poured out the drinks. I opened another story book, and, with an apologetic look in his direction, went into the bedroom and began reading again. Jackie's eyelids remained firmly open. I droned on, occasionally taking a few sips of wine. Two fairy stories and half a bottle of plonk later, she finally went to sleep, as I reached yet another "And they lived happily ever after."

I couldn't help noticing that Everard had risen well to the occasion. As for me, after months of celibacy, and well oiled with wine, I was definitely going to make up for lost time. I threw off my nightie and dressing gown, held in my stomach, thrust out my chest, gave a suggestive wiggle and dived on top of him.

We didn't bother much with foreplay, hungry for sex we passed on the starters and got noisily stuck into the last bit of the first course. My fillings nearly got sucked out as he kissed me passionately and I moaned with delight as he began kissing responsive parts of my body, steadily working southwards. Then we lost all self control and came together for the main course. A couple of good heaves and we were away. The settee shuddered under such punishing action and I began to wonder if I'd ever be able to walk with my knees together again.

As we worked ourselves into frenzy, gathering speed towards the great crescendo, a cross little voice piped up beside us, "What do you think you are doing to my mummy?" Jackie had woken up. Everard, underneath me, instantly deflated. I, one move ahead, was just ready for the final climatic thrust. Nothing could stop it. I banged down with all the force my pelvis could muster. He gasped in pain and grabbed at his battered equipment as we both rolled onto the floor.

"It's all right, it's all right," was all he could say, whilst hastily wrapping his dressing gown around his doubled-over naked body.

Sex was off the menu for the next few days whilst his bruises healed. But once back in action, he was fuel to my now blazing fire. Our rooms were on opposite sides of the building reached by a long corridor that was flanked by bedrooms on each side. With commando-like stealth he would open his door, look, listen, then run like hell to my room. I was always eagerly waiting. But all good things have to come to an end. Bonking, temporarily, had taken precedence over buying, and I felt after this most pleasant interlude, I really should start looking at houses.

Checking out possible properties in estate agents' windows, the descriptions just didn't match the realities. 'Reduced for quick sale,' really meant, 'Someone buy it before it collapses.'

'Semi-detached' – 'Its falling over.'

'No chain involved,' – 'Non-flushing primitive earth toilet down the garden'

'Suit elderly couple,' – 'smells of cabbage and brown Windsor soup.'

'Easy access to the motorway,' – 'it runs along the bottom of the garden.'

'Ten minutes from the sea,' – 'if you ignore higher sea levels and the crumbling cliffs.'

But it didn't take me long to find a neat two-bed roomed ex-council house nearer the business. Situated near parkland, as soon as I walked in I knew that this was 'the one.'

"Do you like it?" I asked Jackie, as we looked around the immaculate interior. We could have just moved in without having to do any work on the building.

"Oh, mummy, I love it," clinched the sale.

Everard and I celebrated our last night together in the "Festival" by consuming a large quantity of wine. He was soon off to Australia. After much passion and a few tears over the parting, he did 'the run' back to his room. Scuttling along as fast as his befuddled state would allow, and in semi-darkness as one of the main lights had gone out, instead of turning left into his bedroom, he turned left too early at the top of the stairs. He fell down thirteen steps, smashed into the glass door at the bottom, which promptly shattered.

The shock sobered him up immediately, and unhurt he raced back to his bedroom before Doug could get his leg on and investigate. It was a sad good-bye to those well filled trousers and good times.

I didn't know it then, but I was heading towards a future where my comfortable life would nosedive into dreadful meltdown and be changed forever.

Bankruptcy And After

The little man with the bald head looked over the top of his glasses at my pin-striped companion and said, "Can we do anything to save this business?"

"No sir," was the sombre reply. Legal jargon floated back and forth between the two, the word bankruptcy being uttered on a number of occasions. Lost in a numb haze, I could only stare at the large, highly polished table between us, property of the County Court, and thought, 'Wow, it must take a cleaner ages to get such a shine on that.' Then it hit me that now I'd lost my business, I could soon be doing such a job to earn some money. I burst into tears. The bald-headed man gave a sympathetic smile, said, "There, there," and handed me a box of paper hankies.

After thirty-eight years of earning a comfortable living from my business, it all fell apart during the commercial crash of the early 1990's. Everything had to be sold to help pay the creditors. I was left with just the house, which at that time, had plummeted into negative equity, and was of no interest to anyone else. However, a large mortgage came with keeping this roof over our heads. I had no idea how I was going to find the money to pay for it, or for that matter, any of the other bills. I had no experience of working for anyone else, no qualifications, and, at fifty-two, menopausal and likely to be nudging into the unemployable age zone. The future looked bleak.

As I locked the now empty pet shop door and drove away for the last time, I couldn't look back. I was saying goodbye to thirty-eight years of my life. Tomorrow would have to be a new beginning. I was dreading that challenge.

"Never mind, mummy," said seven year old Jackie, smiling up at me with the innocence of youth, "You'll be able to spend lots more time with me."

She went to play with a friend; I curled up on the settee and sobbed for everything I had lost. Where was I going from here? Would anyone employ me? A big black emptiness strung out in front of me as depression took over. I went outside and looked at the house. My home, Jackie's inheritance. Frilly curtains, tidy front lawn with pretty flower borders around its edges. I'd worked damned hard to get it, and I wasn't going to give it up without a fight.

"I'm not going to lose you," I said as I reassuringly patted the brickwork, although tears trickled down my face as I stumbled in the front door. Who was I kidding?

Now, I was a single, unemployed parent qualifying for benefits. As much as I didn't want to take the money, preferring to keep supporting myself, I had no other apparent option. After pages of form filling, and a home check to make sure I wasn't fiddling the system or shacking up with a man, the giros started to arrive. There was just enough to pay all the essential bills, although there was little left over at the end of the week. Now classified as 'poor,' I wondered how other neighbours on benefits managed to afford their 50" TVs, big cars and three foreign holidays a year. I soon found out that there was a thriving local 'black market,' where many of them worked for cash in hand and probably didn't have a clue on how to fill out an Income Tax form.

My reduced income resulted in an impoverished new lifestyle. No further bills for gas and electricity would be coming through the letter-box; two key meters were installed instead, which meant higher costs, paid for in advance. BT withdrew its services, because, as a bankrupt, the account could no longer be in my name. One of the trustees of the estate kindly offered to have it transferred into his name until I was free of that debt two years down the line. I couldn't have a bank account with more than £250 in it, and any prospective employer had to be informed of my circumstances. Shame was the name of the game. Even the car had to go. Old and rusty as it was, it might fetch a few pounds to help pay off accumulating administration expenses. A kindly friend put £50 in the kitty, took over the car and gave it back to me. Stock and equipment from the shop had been snapped up at auction for a fraction of its original price.

I had to take on a new mindset and round down my finances. The various bills were now being paid in either weekly or monthly instalments, including a big chunk to The Alliance and Leicester building society. The little left over went towards food. I quickly learnt how to feed ourselves on £10 a week. Instead of microwaveable meals, take - aways or pricey joints of meat, I discovered that potatoes were encouragingly low priced and could be baked, boiled, chipped or fried. Baked beans or tinned spaghetti could be served up cold, thus saving on gas. We did pass on one brand of baked beans costing pennies, when Jackie said in a disgusted voice, "This is like eating rabbit droppings." On one of our lowest days all we had in the fridge was half an old, cold cauliflower. But boiled and served with a splash of salt and pepper it helped to stop our starving tummies from rumbling. Fruit became a healthy and inexpensive pudding. Cheap supermarket 'own brand' bread would just about last the week, although I sometimes had to cut off the crusts by the last day to remove patches of blue mould. By toasting the inner pieces, I squared it with my conscience by telling myself any nasties they might be harbouring would be zapped away in the heat.

My shoes started talking to me as the soles left the uppers and we had to slip thick cardboard into the bottom of Jackie's shiny black school shoes when holes started to appear. We couldn't afford new ones. Charity shops became our preferred source of clothes. Here we discovered that good, branded names could be bought for a tenth of their new retail value. On the plus side, because of my impoverished financial situation, Jackie qualified for free school meals and Council Tax was just £2.00 a month. Like a tiger on the hunt I prowled the supermarkets and shops for perishable foods that were often marked right down just before closing time.

Christmas wasn't far away. This was going to be a difficult time. Presents could no longer be freely bought on a whim, but local charity shops came up trumps with great displays of previously used children's toys. Jackie could have a good time at a reasonable cost.

An ex-customer, seeing me gazing in a shop window, asked how I was getting on.

"Oh, I'm managing," I replied with an unconvincing smile.

"Look," she said, somewhat hesitantly, pulling a piece of paper from her bulky, black handbag, "Will you take this. I don't need it and you might be able to use it." She handed me a £10 voucher for poultry from a local butcher. She would never know what a difference this was going to make to our Christmas when every penny was being counted.

December 25th turned out to be a sunny and almost warm day. Blue skies and fluffy clouds tempted us out for a walk around the park lake. Many others were strolling along, feeding the ducks, sitting on the benches, wishing each other 'Happy Christmas.'

Afterwards, we enjoyed the roast chicken dinner, then Jackie sat in front of the fire and unwrapped her presents.

She looked up at me. "This is the best present, having you all to myself," she said, and I knew we were going to be all right.

The Pet Shop

I waved excitedly to Jackie as she came through the school gates. Taking her hand as we crossed the road to the car, I said, "I've got a job at the other pet shop down the road, isn't that great? We'll have a bit more money coming in now." Her face lit up, "Can I have a paddling pool then?" "We'll see."

Having gone into the pet shop, looking for a friend who worked there, I could barely get in the door because there was a long queue of people waiting to be served. The harassed owner behind the counter was apparently on his own and struggling to serve everyone. He kept pushing up gold-rimmed spectacles that were in danger of sliding off the end of his perspiration laden nose. I took pity on this man who was obviously in all of a dither. As traders we had previously been on a nodding acquaintance so I asked, "David, do you want a hand, I can easily cope?"

"Oh please," he replied, such relief in his voice.

"Just tell me quickly which buttons on the till relate to which products and I'll get stuck in."

I slipped smoothly back into the familiar routine as if it were yesterday. After we'd dealt with the rush, David explained that my friend had been taken to hospital with heart problems and probably wouldn't be coming back to work. As he had Marion as his only other part-time assistant, would I like the job? Would I just.

David was a single man, in his late thirties, an ex-civil servant, whose only previous connection with animals had been as a breeder of budgerigars.

"Why did you buy into this business, it's rather risky after the security of the civil service?" I asked.

He grunted, "I must have been mad at the time."

He was tall and quite handsome, and without his thick

glasses, he couldn't see six inches in front of his face. As it was winter he was wearing a chunky blue jersey with holes in the elbows, a shirt, and unwashed, tatty jeans, which I was convinced, were so grubby they would soon stand up on their own. In summer he just removed the jersey. He had this theory that if customers saw him in better clothes and driving a car newer than his rusty Astra, they might think he was doing far too well and take their business to another pet shop.

In fact, David's pet shop was a little goldmine, in spite of the fact he did not apply business practices that recommended the need to have clean, uncluttered lines of professionally erected shelving, spotlights on special sales areas, up-to-the-minute technology to weigh out goods, and eye-catching shop logos on all the carrier bags.

The shop did indeed have shelves, rough wooden ones of varying length and height.

"Where did you get those from?" I asked.

"Local tips and skips," he proudly replied, "Saved me a bomb in costs."

The spotlights aimed on the special sales areas were non-existent, because David had never got round to buying any new bulbs, so just the empty shades were angled towards the bargain products.

The electronic scales would have had an inspector from the Trading Standards Office pulling his hair out. Held together with chunky bits of sticky tape, it occasionally had a brainstorm, throwing up incorrect weights and prices on the front panel, where the tiny lights in this section seemed to form a malevolent sneer.

"You'll have to get an engineer in to put this right," I said to David the first time I pressed the buttons and it had a funny turn.

"No," he replied, "We give it percussive maintenance, which is the fine art of whacking the crap out of it to get it working again."

We also had bags with eye-catching logos, recycled ones from Tesco's, Sainsbury's and Waitrose.

Incoming products were never dealt with in a logical sequence, just stacked into any spare spaces. I had a neat and tidy mind and spent ages re-arranging and putting all like products together, only to find that David had dumped them back in a heap, because, according to his methods, "I can't sort out the weekly orders because I don't know where anything is."

Trying to keep everything clean was another problem; there was an embarrassment of dead moths and spiders in the window and a layer of dust everywhere. The cleaning utensils consisted of one filthy duster, one broom with a few straggly bristles and two brushes, like balding hedgehogs, tucked into a broken handled dustpan.

His money saving efforts kept us short on toilet rolls, washing up liquid and bleach. In the tiny kitchen area hung a blue towel. This was for drying our hands after we'd washed them in cold water. There wasn't any hot water – he'd disconnected that. The towel never got washed. At the beginning of each week David would give it a quarter turn, presenting a dry end at the bottom ready for use. It got rougher and rougher, holes began to appear in the faded cotton, but he kept on turning it. In desperation, I gave him a new one as a Christmas present.

His 'office' was a tiny back room, where he would sit at a ramshackle old desk methodically checking each invoice. Typical of an ex-civil servant, all the paperwork was gone through in triplicate.

Outside, at the rear, there were a few dilapidated, empty rabbit hutches leaning against a double garage. This building was used as a store and contained sacks of corn and seeds, all stacked on pallet boards just inside the door. Bales of hay and straw were behind and right at the back was a heap of assorted items occupying a space, which could be labelled 'if you don't know what to do with it, dump here.' On opening the door various unpleasant smells wafted out – of damp, rotten wood and wet straw, mouldy seeds, all interwoven with the pungent aroma of resident rats.

"David, you're going to have to get rid of them, they're trouble."

He turned a whiter shade of pale and reluctantly took a packet of poison from off the sales shelf. This was a cheaper option than getting in a pest controller. But given the choice between the poison or the pet foods, the rats opted to consume the latter, stuffed their faces and continued to multiply.

This garage had a rickety door that was left open in the daytime; at night David carefully padlocked it, oblivious to the fact that the one and only hinge was held on by three rusty screws and a bent nail, no deterrent to thieves. He did look at it with renewed interest when I cynically observed, "That could probably qualify for the Antiques Road Show."

Spotting a racing pigeon sunning itself on the shed roof I asked, "What's that big, fat pigeon doing up there?"

"We call him 'Lucky.' According to the address stamped under his wing, he hails from Bristol. He turned up one day, discovered free bed and board, and stayed. Occasionally I'll box him up and hand him to any of the delivery drivers heading west, with instructions to let him out a good few miles down the road, hoping he will then fly on to his owner. But a few hours after departure we'll always find that 'Lucky' has boomeranged back to the garage roof."

I did wonder if this plump bird was going to be David's cost-free Christmas dinner. I visualised Lucky laid out, feet skywards, with balls of stuffing stuck in various orifices. But this possibility never materialised, because one day the bird decided, during the rush hour, to wolf down the remains of a discarded sandwich tossed into the middle of the main road. All that was left of unlucky 'Lucky', after a double-decker bus sped by, was a splodge on the tarmac and a few grey feathers flying around in the wind.

The shop had a large forecourt and when spring arrived, David pulled out from the back of the garage a tall, multi-shelved trolley which we loaded up with hundreds of colourful geraniums, fuchsias and bedding plants and wheeled it out of the shop in the morning and back in at night. But it was from the school of Scrapheap Challenge, and had a major design fault –no brakes.

One morning, when there was a near gale-force wind blowing, I tried to wrestle the heavy trolley into its right location, and anchor its wheels with compost bags. But the forces were far too great, a hearty gust of tornado proportions wrenched the unit from my grasp and I could only watch in horror as it careered swiftly away along the pavement, shedding its cargo of pots, trays and flowers. An unsuspecting driver, having just parked his large shiny black car nearby, suddenly spotted this mobile garden heading ominously towards him and his vehicle. On reaching the edge of the kerb the trolley toppled over; there was a loud crunch as it whacked the front bumper of his BMW into a new shape and spattered colourful flowers all over the body-work

David threw up his hands in horror. "What on earth were you doing?" he shouted at me and couldn't apologise enough to the angry driver. In shock, all I kept muttering was, "I couldn't help it, I couldn't hold it," and expected to be out of a job on the spot.

But I wasn't, although I was barred from pushing the trolley out any more. He had to shell out £300 for bodywork repairs. I don't know if he put in a successful insurance claim, but probably not, as a few days later he upped the price of every bird and animal cage by two pounds.

Left beside the now well - anchored trolley were two large boxes with a notice about saving the planet and re-cycling flower pots and bedding plant trays. Loyal customers would bring along these items, and when the boxes were filled, David would remove the original notices and put a new one up with '5p each.'

The front of the shop badly needed painting; some of the frame was so rotten that the large glass window was in danger of falling out. The wooden door had also warped over the years. During the winter the wood swelled and customers had to give it a hefty kick to get in. When it got to the point of sticking fast, David started panicking at the possibility of a diminishing customer base and got a carpenter's plane with a blunt blade to try to scrape off the surplus wood. Over the years, he'd had to do this each winter, and come summer, as the wood dried out and shrunk, we got a fearful draught whistling through the gap.

Just inside this door, the constant footfall periodically opened up a hole in the concrete floor and crumpled bits of lino fell into it, followed by angry customers threatening compensation for twisted ankles. One mother, pushing a baby buggy, tripped into this ever widening cavity, and as she fell over she lost her grip on the pram. It shot across the floor, hit the side of the guinea-pig pen and deposited her unstrapped offspring in amongst the scattering animals. By the time she had regained her composure her baby had learnt two new lessons in life. Guinea-pig poo tastes awful, but has fascinating and exceptional adhesive qualities. Fearful of having to part with any money, David turned on all the charm he could muster and when she had gone he raked out an old box of filler from the back of the shed and lobbed a bit of the mixture into the hole.

With no proper stock rotation, deliveries were often dumped on the top of previously delivered goods, and some of the grains that had been around a while began to show signs of insect activity. These would appear as maggots in the early stage and then turn into small, fluffy, mushroom coloured moths. On departing from their granary homes they would leave a legacy of fine, sticky webbing woven into the seeds, and the ceiling would be smothered in a layer of newly emerged moths. Rather than lose money by killing them with pest sprays sold in the shop, David would go round whacking at them violently with rolled up newspapers, which cracked the false ceiling tiles and gave us the unwelcome job of sweeping up the numerous corpses with the straggly bristle broom and balding hedgehog brushes.

David fostered this image of thriftiness with a touch of pride. We always joked that he sobbed when he had to pay the Inland Revenue, and he went decidedly white when presented with any bills. Important ones were reluctantly paid, but he could never be persuaded to stump up for essential repairs.

A prime example of this was a plastic and wooden structure, attached, loosely, to the rear of the building. It was laughingly called a 'lean to'. 'Falling down' would have been more appropriate. It had a breezeblock base which came up to waist level, large plastic windows and sheets of cracked corrugated plastic on the roof, which let in buckets of water every time it rained. The door was coming off its hinges, and had dropped down so much that every time it was opened, there were nasty scraping noises as one end scratched out a half circular channel in the crumbling concrete.

During the winter, the floor was constantly wet, and the cat litter stored out there soaked up all this moisture and turned into a soggy mess. David, penny pinching again, filled up the holes in the roof with strips of polystyrene he had broken off old bedding plant trays, but to no avail. Water still trickled in; the cans of pet food turned rusty, and the grass seed started to sprout in its sack. I lost the sale of an expensive dog coat when I pulled it out of its crumpled plastic wrapper and poured half a pint of filthy water all over the customer's newly clipped white poodle. I blew my top.

"Why don't you smarten this place up a bit? If you put some money into it you'd surely increase your turnover, it's got to be a worthwhile investment. All of this is making me a nervous wreck. I never know when I pull out a packet of bird seed whether I'm going to find a large spider attached to it, or worse, a mouse inside. The stuff in that lean-to is all spoiling, there's rats still multiplying in the garage and the front door is sticking again. And - you've also got a death-trap of electrical wiring behind the counter; it's got A & E written all over it." A six socket cable tidy was laid on the floor just below the till. Into it was fed cables from a multitude of appliances. To try and stop anyone from tripping over them, David had covered them with another hazard, a dust-laden piece of old carpet with curled up edges. I could not understand why he was reluctant to spend any money on this business, although I was to find out in due course.

Because David was youngish bachelor, quite good looking with his own profitable business, he constantly attracted a steady stream of interested, man-hunting females who tried to work their feminine charms on him, often by buying items their pets didn't really need. As he smiled and nodded, they dipped further into their purses. Marion and I, being both older and wiser, often looked on with amusement.

"Watch this one," I said, as an attractive blonde with high heels tried a great deal of eyelash fluttering towards David's smiling face. He was definitely going to get some financial mileage out of her. "Good Morning and how are you today?" he enquired in his best money extracting voice. She, rising to his charms, bought a couple of items, and then, in the mistaken belief that she might have scored, bought some more pet food and accessories, obviously hoping to keep the conversation going towards a satisfactory ending. But, David, having totted up her well – into - double - figures bill, smilingly took the bundle of twenty pound notes and dumped the goods in a heap on the counter.

"Thank you," he said, passing over her change and receipt. She gave him her brightest smile and waited, hopefully.

We both knew what was following. "Bet you he let's her carry that lot out to the car herself," muttered Marion.

"Yup, I think you're right," I replied as blonde lady stood there, obviously hoping for some gentlemanly help and maybe more. David did get up, but only to open the shop door wide enough for her to stagger through with her arms full of packages.

Other females, being cannier, tried the old ploy, "The way to a man's heart is through his stomach." Everyone knew David didn't do cooking, as in his flat over the shop he didn't possess a cooker or microwave. He reckoned that as he spent the majority of his time working at the business, the only necessary items up there were a bed and a TV, which was balanced on an old wooden crate. He bought all his meals out. We said he must have shares in the café opposite, as he patronised them twice a day, every day.

One of the café assistants took a shine to him, and began giving him bigger portions. He capitalised on this for ages until she started sitting down 'to keep him company' whilst he ate. David was an ardent football fan and, at lunchtime each day, avidly read the sports page of the Daily Mail (borrowed from me, he never bought his own.) He got stuck in a catch 22 situation. If he buried himself in the paper, she might get huffy and probably dock his food, and if he encouraged her, heaven knows what might happen? His little world, organised by his standards, was now not running the way he wished. He became snappy and moody as he couldn't go anywhere else nearby for food. This café was the nearest and most convenient place. So he switched to the min - market next door, buying ready - made pre - packed sausage rolls and pies. But one of the assistants here, thinking he had changed shops because he fancied her, came on strong each day as he walked through the door.

His salvation came in the form of Kerry, a lovely, large, cheerful lady who lived nearby. She fancied her chances with David and got streets ahead of the competition by bringing in her ready cooked meals. She was a brilliant cook and craftily asked David, "Will you give me your verdict on some new recipes I'm trying out?" Not only was it wonderful food, she came with regular supplies and made no obvious demands on him.

And David nearly succumbed. Wooed by a succession of spicy stews, home made quiches, roast dinners and sherry trifles, he loosened up towards Kerry and we would find them having long intense conversations together. But some of the gloss went off the relationship the day David returned a large pile of crockery to Kerry that was unwashed and sprouting furry patches. I think she then realised that David was not cut out to be husband material, so she settled for a good friend. She even managed to persuade him to buy a new pair of jeans, but just to keep up the impecunious image, he still wore the grubby, holey jersey.

Then the phone calls started. Mysterious ones, when you picked up the phone there was no-one there. We joked about it being another lady friend David didn't want us to know about. Other times a refined female voice would ask for, "Mr Sutton, please," and David would say,

"I'll take it on the upstairs phone." And he'd disappear to the flat for ages. Marion and I would nudge each other and wink when he came down, but he wouldn't let on who it was. He seemed quite happy to let us think he was stringing along another female. Little did we know what he was really up to.

October came around again; I'd been working at the pet shop for over a year and had settled into a pleasant routine. The mortgage was being paid on a regular basis, as were the other bills, I even started to try and save for a newer car, putting away the odd ten or twenty pounds into a bank account.

David had a birthday due; he insisted it was his thirty-ninth. "No, it's not," said Kerry, "It's your fortieth." David visibly blanched. Kerry, in one of her wickedly mischievous moods, decided that this landmark should not go unrecorded and began to plot 'a surprise.'

She lay in wait for me as I left work and said, "How about if we come back later in the evening and paint "Happy 40th Birthday David," right across the shop window, embellished with a big bunch of balloons?"

"I think he'd kill the pair of us, as he'd know exactly who'd done it," I replied.

Kerry didn't seem to think this would even be enough. She had visions of doing much bigger and better things for this celebration. Because she was privy to more of David's confidences than anyone else, I didn't realise there was more to this than just a birthday celebration.

With a week to spare, she came up with the idea of a party. Not any old party, but a real whiz bang of a do.

"How on earth are you going to get it ready on time?" I queried.

"No problem, you just leave it to me," she giggled. "Go and invite all of his friends. Tell them it's my place Saturday night, 8pm, bring a bottle, and to keep their mouths shut."   As David was not a social animal, there was the enormous problem of dragging him away from either his business or his television on a Saturday night.

"I've got it all planned," laughed Kerry, her large frame wobbling away.

During that week, Kerry's sister made a 'Pamela Anderson' cake, suitably iced with a tan-coloured, shapely reclining nude, sporting upwardly thrusting breasts, and including all the naughty bits. But we then chickened out and iced on a dotted yellow bikini. And to add to the fun we hired a stripper who was going to bring a racy Kissogram. We chortled away to ourselves as we tried to imagine how David would handle such a situation, his social life did need spicing up, and here was a fantastic birthday treat for him.

But we still had to get him out of his flat on Saturday night. M15 would have been proud of our subterfuge. We deliberately let David believe we were plotting something, but he had no idea the range of celebrations.

Friend Nick, who shared his love of football, they'd occasionally watch a match together, asked David if he'd like to go out for a curry dinner on Saturday night. This prised David out of his flat, and, as they drove along, Nick did some jiggery-pokery with the dials on the dashboard, causing the engine to cough and glide silently to a halt, conveniently outside Kerry's house. All our vehicles were hidden around the back, giving nothing away.

"Oh dear," said Nick, when he'd had a quick look under the bonnet, "I can't fix this, I'll have to ring for a taxi as the table's booked for 8pm." This was a time before mobile phones, so, "Look, we're right outside Kerry's house, I'll see if I can use her phone to tell the curry house we'll be late, and order a taxi."

In a dim and silent house some thirty people sat quietly giggling at the set-up. The floor had been cleared, balloons hung up, numerous bottles congregated on the sideboard and the table groaned under the weight of all the party food, including the cleaned up version of the 'Pamela Anderson' cake.

Nick came in, grinning. "He's out in the car." A small cheer went up. "I'll have to stay here a minute or two, as he thinks I'm making a couple of phone calls. Then I'll go and tell him the taxi will be about fifteen minutes and Kerry's invited us in for a quick coffee."

After a few minutes, David and Nick walked in. The lights went on, everyone clapped.

"Happy birthday to you, happy birthday to you," we chorused, our glasses raised.

David blinked behind his glasses, like an owl caught in a flashlight.

"You rotters, I knew something was up."

But he smiled and was persuaded to sit down. Someone thrust a filled glass into his hand. The music came on; we began to dance and enjoy the food and drink.

"I didn't know you were doing this all for me," said David to those around him. We smiled Cheshire cat smiles and thought 'You haven't got to the best bit yet.' He refused hard alcohol, and sat sipping lemonade. Kerry short-circuited this pooper by slyly lacing all the following drinks with generous splashes of vodka. After half –an - hour, David, now tie - less, was pleasantly mellowed and somewhat flushed.

The door bell rang and a voice called out, "David, it's for you." Getting to his feet, but listing a bit to starboard, he took a few wobbly steps towards the front door and was greeted by the 46" bust of a Kissogram cowgirl. His mouth dropped open and a strangled gargle came out. She was six feet tall, dressed in a fringed leather outfit that didn't cover up much of her shapely, bronzed body. Long legs that went up to her armpits and a cowboy hat perched on top of a mane of chestnut hair. David took his glasses off, polished them, put them back on and had a good look.

"There you are," said Kerry, "That's your birthday present. She's come to give you a very happy birthday."

Kissogram girl's male assistant put on some music. The sound of The Stripper blared around the room as she picked up a small whip with little leather thongs. David gulped and took two steps back.

"I hear you've been a naughty boy, David," she said, lightly whacking her hands with the thongs. David took two more steps back. Beads of perspiration were breaking out on his forehead.

"Right, you have been a naughty boy, get down on your hand and knees, you got to be punished." The whip cracked in the air. Cornered, David did as he was told.
"I'm going to give you ten lashes on your bottom for being naughty, and everyone is going to count them."

The whip descended. "One, two, and three..." We entered into the spirit of things and chanted along, "... eight, nine, and ten."

She stopped. A plaintive voice from beneath her straddled legs, said, "That's only nine. More, I want more." David, aided by the best part of a half a bottle of vodka, had really entered into the spirit of things.

As the music throbbed on, he got unsteadily to his feet and rocked gently as he was assailed by a curvaceous body rubbing up against him. He was persuaded to remove his shirt, shoes and socks, and stood there looking decidedly silly with his index fingers covering each nipple. He swiftly removed them when she made a sneaky bid to unzip his trousers. A small struggle went on as she pulled down and he pulled up.

Undeterred at undressing him, she began to remove her own gear. Off came the fringed jacket and the 46" of upwardly thrusting bust, barely contained in a black, lacy bra, came into view. A few more wriggles and off came the skirt, revealing a tiny thong, plus every man's delight, a black suspender belt. She lifted up one stockinged leg, and, with the toe of her pointed shoe, teasingly slid it up his leg. He grabbed it at high thigh level, and gazed in fascination as she slowly undid the suspenders. He started to stroke her leg with a great deal of enthusiasm when she peeled off her stockings. Her assistant then handed her a plastic rose, which she promptly tucked into her ample cleavage, where its red head nodded and beckoned.

A look of delight spread across David's face as she tied his hands behind his back and invited him the remove the rose from its enticing location. A liberal spread of honey on the glistening skin only added to his delight. He lunged forward, eager to bury himself between the soft twin peaks. As he did so, she leaned back. His outstretched tongue lapped up a drop of honey when he excitedly dived in for his prize. But, befuddled by alcohol, his aim was off centre, he fell forward and the two of them ended up in a wriggling heap on the floor. His face disappeared into the depths of the black bra. We yelled triumphantly as he reluctantly came up for air, clutching the rose in his teeth. His glasses had got lost in this voluptuous valley.

But the show was not yet over. There were yet more goodies to come for David. After untying his hands, the stripper gyrated around him as he slowly got up, rubbing her tight and cellulite-free bum up against his trousers. He grabbed his waistband in a firm grip as once again she tried to de-bag him. Undeterred, she faced him and did a few hip rotations to keep his interest up, whilst removing his glasses from the depths of black lace.

David squinted, without his glasses he couldn't see further than six inches before everything became blurred. With a flourish, accompanied by a loud roar from us, she deftly whipped off her bra and her large breasts dropped considerably nearer to her naval. Not being able to see what was going on, David stood there with a silly smile on his face.

The stripper stood beside him, waiting, unused to such hesitation. She nudged his thigh with her shoe and he rocked slightly. His face had gone beetroot red, his hands still tightly gripping the top of his trousers. In spite of his protests, she managed to prise off one hand and planted it firmly right in the middle of her volumous womanly flesh. David squeezed and a great big smile spread across face.

"I like this," he said, having a good grope. She gave him back his glasses and with one hand he hastily put them on to have a better look. His other hand was still in its resting place.

"Cor," he muttered in admiration, "Bloody lovely," And fell in a befuddled heap on the floor. Spark out. We hauled him into the nearest armchair and left him there.

The party went on until about 1 am, when we all went home. David, by that time had recovered enough to finish off the other half of the vodka bottle, still thinking the lemonade was a bit strong. He managed to walk home by himself, insisting he needed some fresh air, and crashed out, being woken at midday by Kerry, who became worried because his curtains were still drawn. He couldn't recall much of the previous evening.

"Never mind," said Kerry, "We've got it all on tape."

Nick had borrowed a video recorder and filmed the lot. The raunchy stripper, the bare boobs, the alcoholic haze. Every bit of it recorded for posterity. Unfortunately not being used to this piece of equipment, he'd held it upside down, so when it was screened you could only see it properly if you stood on your head. But it was a great talking point for months afterwards, and I heard a few copies were made.

I went to work on Monday, and as I cleaned out the rabbits, said, "Did you enjoy the party?" He'd still got shadows under his eyes and was moving around carefully.

"And did you like your birthday present?"

By then he'd seen the video. He visibly squirmed, mumbled, "Yes," and found himself a job to do. Raking out the rabbit's food dish that it had been using as a toilet and thinking that 'shit shoveller' really didn't sit comfortably with my job description of shop assistant, I said, "I don't know how we're going to top this for your next birthday."

He came back and looked at me. A funny look. I suddenly felt uncomfortable. Something was wrong. He shuffled his feet.

"I don't know how to put this, Kerry told me that I should have spoken to you before now, but I couldn't find the courage to say anything. I've sold the business; the new owners are taking over next week. Kerry's known for a long time, but I swore her to secrecy. That party was also a goodbye one. I'm going to America, to Florida. I'm sorry; there won't be a job for you after the end of this week."

The Car

So, once again money was short. I was terrified that something would go wrong with the car, because I couldn't really afford to have it repaired. It was an essential part of our lives, such as getting Jackie to school and I needed it to go job hunting. Bus fares were far too pricy.

My heart sank when the dreaded time came around for the yearly MOT, and John, the garage mechanic, gazed sympathetically at my rust riddled vehicle and noisily sucked in his breath.

"It's 'er emissions. You won't likely get her through the MOT this time."

My 'Tin Lizzie' gave another cough and her exhaust belched a cloud of black smoke thick enough to stop shipping in the English Channel. I knew that she already had one wheel in the gates of the Great Breaker's Yard in the Sky, but I couldn't send her there just yet.

"What's wrong with it then?" I asked.

"Probably afraid to go out," remarked Jackie cynically as we stood gazing at the car's dented bonnet, lop sided bumper and two tone colours of deep blue and rust. 'Tin Lizzie' was a hybrid car, with more replaced parts than the six million dollar man, a skip on wheels. I'd certainly never get a speeding ticket; it was a miracle if she got to the top of a steep hill. The only way she'd reach 60 miles an hour would be if I drove her off Beachy Head.

Desperately hoping this visit wasn't going to cost too much, I enquired, "Well, for a start, do you have a windscreen wiper for this car?"

John laughed and jokingly said, "Sounds like a fair swap to me."

Any expenditure on tin Lizzie was financially challenging, so to help get her through the MOT at a reasonable price, I had to try and obtain a second-hand thingamajig from the car breaker's yard. Black and greasy, it bore a passing resemblance to a dead octopus. Once fitted, it also worked just about as efficiently as one. The emissions were worse. The engine now sounded like an army tank. Jackie dived to the floor when we passed any of her friends. When cyclists began to overtake us, she said, "That's it, I'm walking to school."

I gave in, and having raided my pathetic savings account, took 'Lizzie' back to the garage. The emissions turned out to be the least of my worries. When she was hoisted up on a hydraulic lift, it exposed a whole new world looking at her workings from underneath. John thrust his screwdriver into rusty orifices, teasing out bits of four-year-old "Daily Star" strung together with body filler.

"Well," he said, "You are going to need..." He reeled off a lengthy list. I swallowed hard.

I'd loved to have had enough savings to afford a newer car, something fast and flashy that did 0-60 in a few short seconds. I really fancied a Cabriolet, often advertised for those who like the wind in their hair. But with 'Lizzie', we got that at no extra cost. Her windows were always falling down whenever we went over any bumps. Many vehicles have air bags; we'd got sick bags in ours. I loved the smell of new upholstery, which was such a pleasant change from the permanent pong of damp clothes and a mouldy apple core that had rolled into an irretrievable corner. Quality covers sadly didn't mix with a child whose hands were permanently welded to bottles of fizzy cherryade. Our dappled, pale pink seats looked quite... well, individual.

I scraped up enough money to pay the garage and 'Lizzie' got her MOT. I breathed a sigh of relief, and as a special treat put her through the car wash. This was wonderful; here we were back on the road again. I hitched out her choke, tethered it with a clothes peg, and purred along to the shopping centre to stock up on cheap baked beans.

As I emerged from the revolving door, I saw Jackie waving from the car park. I waved back.

"Mum, mum," she cried out.

"Yes, dear," I replied, mentally checking that I hadn't forgotten anything.

"Oh mum, someone's just reversed into poor old Lizzie and put another dent in her bumper."

Having got financial settlement for repairs from the guilty and embarrassed driver, all was well in the mechanical world, until a few days before Christmas. The car suddenly developed a strange whistle when moving. I had a quick look under the bonnet just in case I could see anything that was obviously disconnected or broken, but all appeared to be in order. So, with hazard lights flashing, I slowly drove to the garage to see if my friendly mechanic could help.

"Sorry, love" said John, "I'm fully booked up until after the Holidays. It might be a slipping fan belt."

"No, I know what at slipping fan belt sounds like, this is more of a whistle than a squeak."

"Whatever it is, I'll have to check it out next week."

With hazard lights again in action, I slowly drove home, hoping the car didn't pack up on the way. I discovered that when the speed was below thirty miles an hour, the noise stopped.

Having parked outside my house I opened up the bonnet again to see if I could spot the problem. A useless action, but one born of desperation. However, the sight of one female peering into mechanical depths acted as a magnet to three of my male neighbours.

David, from across the road, nonchalantly strolled over.

"Got a problem, then?" He too, peered into the depths of the engine.

"There's a squeak."

"A squeak – probably a slipping fan belt, needs tightening up."

"No, I know what a slipping fan belt sounds like; this is more of a whistle."

From two doors down Peter emerged, armed with a hammer and a screwdriver.

"Can I help?"

"I've got a squeak in the engine."

"Probably a slipping fan belt, then."

"No this is more of a whistle than a squeak."

"Got to be the alternator, then."

"How long does a dodgy alternator last?" I tentatively enquired, hoping it would hold together until the next week."

"How long is a piece of string?" said Peter.

Andy, Peter's neighbour, joined the little gang.

"What's the problem?"

"There's a squeak in the engine, and it's not a slipping fan belt."

"Well, it might just possibly be a failing water pump then, but I wouldn't be sure."

All three were now totally immersed in finding out what was causing this mysterious noise. Tools and tool boxes were hauled out of sheds and vehicles, oil stained overalls donned, and I could only stand uselessly by, hoping that one of them might come up with an answer. But, although they spent ages poking, prodding and exchanging comments, they couldn't find the cause of this whistling gremlin.

"Look, I suggest that we all pile in and go for a run, and then you can hear this noise."

Once onto the dual carriageway I carefully nudged the speed up to forty miles an hour. As I did, a thin, reedy whistle started.

"The wind's blowing through a gap somewhere," said

Peter, the others agreed, and checked out whether all the windows were completely shut.

"I think it's coming from that vent in front of you," observed Andy, "I bet you've got a leaf stuck in there somewhere."

We turned the fan up to full and wiggled a few levers to try and blow this leaf out, but with no success.

Once home, the three of them quickly removed the dashboard in their enthusiastic hunt for this wayward leaf.

"Well, this is a bit of a mystery," said Peter, "Maybe we ought to do a bit of lateral thinking. Perhaps the wind is whistling through a small rust hole in one of your doors."

This was a strong possibility, given the disintegrating state of the car; there could even be a selection of various sized rust spots to choose from. All four doors were opened, a few holes discovered, and Peter carefully applied some filler.

Six cups of tea later followed by a speedy run down the main road and everyone admitted defeat. The whistling continued.

The following week, as I delivered the car to the garage, I told John all about the in - depth investigating we'd done. Two hours later I got a phone call to say he'd solved the problem. When he handed me the car keys there was a smile on his face that could only be likened to a cat that's got the cream.

"Well, go on," I urged, "Tell me what it was."

"Quite a challenge," he admitted as he held up something for me to see.

"Here's the cause of your problem. The wind was whistling through this bit of parcel tape that had got stuck to your wing mirror."

The Sandwich Bar

I scoured the 'JOBS' section of the local paper to see if there was anything interesting that I could cope with. I knew a lot about pets, but not much else. And any job that I took needed to fit around school hours.

In this part of the country, often jokingly referred to as 'Costa Geriatricia,' the numerous rest homes catering for the elderly were always needing carers, but, I couldn't see myself as a bedpan lady. Hotel chambermaid, well, maybe. Shop assistant in a bakery, now that was interesting. I liked working behind a counter and having a bit of a chat with the customers. The hours were suitable, 9-2, five days a week. When school holidays came around, I knew that a friend who did childcare could look after Jackie.

I phoned the number and a voice with a strong accent said, "Who dat?"

"I'm phoning about the shop assistant's job."

"Oh, yes, yes, come, come, we will talk about it."

It was a busy bakery and tea rooms on a main road. Displayed in the big windows I could see cabinets full of jam and chocolate doughnuts, cream cakes, crusty loaves, and soft, melt in the mouth bread baps. I felt I'd put on half a pound just looking at this mouth watering food. From inside the delicious aroma of freshly percolated coffee hit my nostrils.

All around there were customers sitting at tables eating from big plates filled with a variety of popular fast foods; a queue was waiting at the counter to buy the still hot bread as it came from the bake house next door. I studied a glass cabinet containing a selection of high tiered wedding cakes; another had children's birthday iced sponges, fashioned into teddy bears and steam engines. My mouth began to water. If I got this job, I hoped samples of this scrumptious food might be one of the perks.

A girl behind the counter dispensing teas and coffees directed me to a partially open door with the word 'Office' on it. Inside I could see a hunched figure reading a newspaper, seated at a huge desk.

I politely knocked. "Coma in." I did as I was told. "Sita down." I sat down. Mr. Bellini was small, rotund and balding, wearing big framed glasses that distorted his eyes.

He talked. His Italian accent was so difficult to follow I found myself nodding and smiling at parts of the conversation I couldn't understand. But it did appear that I'd got the job, with two week's paid holiday. I started the following Thursday. But not at the bakery. He was opening a sandwich bar on one of the busy main roads up to the seafront and I'd got the job of manageress for the summer season, although I wouldn't be overseeing any staff - I was the only staff. We shook hands to seal the deal.

He lost interest in me and slumped back in his comfy chair behind the desk, intently studying a couple of television screens being fed by security cameras sited in the shop.

As I gleefully passed the counter, the girl asked, "Did you get the job?"

"Yes," I replied, grinning with pleasure. She sniffed.

"You don't know what you've let yourself in for," and began savagely stabbing at the baked potatoes with a thin, sharp knife.

The sandwich bar was on the ground floor of a tatty, three storey, Victorian building near the seafront. I had heard that the property had been bought at a knockdown price with the intention of renovating the two flats above and selling them at a profit. For many years the previous owner of the shop had sold clothes for women of 'a certain age.' But as time went by, and sixty became the 'new forty,' the styles modelled by the headless plaster manikins in the window went right out of fashion. The shop failed to move with the times and closed down.

Now it was to become a retail food outlet, catering for the hoards of visitors heading for the beach. To catch this lucrative summer trade, this shop had to be up and running as soon as possible. Summoned on a Wednesday for the induction, I met Steve, who was to give me all the necessary information. He confessed that he didn't want to be working on what was 'his day off', so all I got was a hurried tour around two large, empty glass display units, a floor to ceiling fridge plus a chill cabinet full of cold drinks.

He explained, "Trays of rolls, bread, pasties and cakes will be delivered here first thing in the morning and left behind the shutters. The ingredients for making up filled roll orders are in the big fridge. Keep it all clean. A full list of prices is by the till and someone will be along by 2pm each day to collect the takings.

With that, he gave me a key for the front door, an emergency contact number and told me to start at nine the following morning. As I was going to be there on my own I thought the owners would have had everything sorted. It didn't quite turn out like that.

Next morning, after dropping Jackie off at the nearby school, I parked the car and decided to walk along the seafront to the shop. The sun was shining, the beach was filling up with visitors, and life began to feel good. I'd got a job and could stop worrying about debts, bills and permanent shortage of cash. Didn't someone say that life was like riding a bicycle, as long as you keep pedalling, you won't fall off? The wheels were certainly turning well for me, I just hoped that life's brakes were not going to be needed.

I arrived outside the shop, looked at the building

and took a deep breath. This was to be my domain for the summer. But, what I had not seen yesterday was a massive portcullis of a security grille that would have repelled invaders to a medieval castle. I was shut out of my little kingdom without a key and the emergency number was inside. What a start to the day. I'd have to walk through town to their next shop to get help.

Behind the grille, and in front of the recessed door, I could see the delivery driver had dropped off a tall stack of trays filled with food for the day. Maybe I didn't need a key for this heap of old iron after all. I bent down and gave the rusty metal a hitch. It moved upwards half an inch. I tried again, but the grille, buckled and crinkled with age, creaked up another quarter inch and stuck. I became aware that a number of curious, but unhelpful people were watching me as I fruitlessly struggled with the unyielding ironwork, breaking off most of my fingernails. I could feel my face starting to flush with embarrassment.

An old lady pushing a wicker shopping trolley stopped to watch and shouted out, "Give it a good kicking at the bottom, love, that's what I've seen them do when I've gone by." Magic. With a hefty kick that bruised my toes and left my feet numb inside my ancient Hush Puppies, I managed to free the grille and push it up. As I hobbled forward, unlocked the front door and dragged in the stack of food trays, the small crowd, like lemmings, followed.

Then I discovered there wasn't a light switch beside the door, where it ought to be. Steve hadn't told me about this. Where was it? I hunted around in desperation, trying to make sense of the Spaghetti Junction of electrical cables snaking behind the drink's cabinet. Logic told me they must lead to some switches.

"Can you give me a couple of Cornish pasties, love?" enquired a member of the now rapidly swelling crowd, "I've got to get back to work."

Others close behind him also muttered their needs for

food in a hurry, so after consulting the price list, I started selling the sticky buns, loaves and rolls straight out of the crates. Because there was no power, the till was unusable, so I opened my purse and tried to give change from its scant contents.

A helpful customer, noting the lack of light problem, traced the switches to behind the drinks cabinet, and the strip-lights flickered on. A cheer went up from the now diminishing queue. Over came a five pound note for a doughnut and I pinged open the till, pleased at last that we were seeing some action. But inside the drawer all I found were a few five pence pieces and a couple of fifty pence. All I could say to the hovering crowd was, "Sorry, folks, can you try and give me the right money, as I've got little change in the till."

The shop began to resemble the interior of a small bank, as notes and coins were traded between customers, pockets were dug deeply and purses emptied out. Within a short time I had taken a reasonable amount of money from just selling the food from the stacked trays.

One member of the queue wanted her money's worth.

"Do you bake the loaves here?"

"No, they come from the main bakery."

"Is it a good bakery?"

"Yes."

Is it soft bread inside?"

"Yes, the farmhouse bread is crisp on the outside, soft on the inside."

"Can you slice it for me to see?"

"Sorry we don't have a slicing machine here."

"Do you know if the bakery down the road has one?"

"Sorry, I don't."

"Oh well, I'll have to ask my husband then."

In a quiet moment, I dialled the emergency number, which was the main shop further into town.

"I have a bit of a problem here, I desperately need

plenty of change, and there was none left in the till. Can you help me out as soon as possible?"

"Of course," came the heartening reply, "Someone will be down shortly." Empty promises, I was left to get on with things as best as I could.

Having sorted my way through the original rush, I began setting out the cake and roll display in the window. It was a fantastically sunny day, the holidaymakers were gathering in interested groups looking at the chocolate éclairs, iced rings and Danish pastries that I had invitingly arranging in their plastic cases.

But, as the hot sun climbed higher in the sky, the heat pouring in through the glass, began to melt the icing. It slowly slid off the cakes and began to form sticky pools in the trays. I nipped outside to see if there was a sunblind that I could pull down for some shade. There was, but no sign of a suitable hooked pole stacked away in a corner of the shop. But I did find a broom with a large head and tried to prise the blind out with this. But brooms were not designed as pulling agents for reluctant blinds. As I tugged hard, the head snapped off, did a whirring half circle up in the air and disappeared into the crowded street. I heard a yelp of pain, followed by some angry shouting, so, clutching the handle, I decided to make myself scarce before the injured party came looking for someone to blame. The redesigned cakes were dumped in the chill cabinet and labelled "Cook's mishaps – half price."

By 11am the morning rush had finished, so before the midday one began, I thought that I had better check on the kitchen area and the now urgently required toilet facilities. From the bangs and crashes above, I knew work was still progressing in the flats upstairs. But when I opened the kitchen door I found a gaping hole in the ceiling and a layer of thick white dust on every surface. In the middle of the room lay a heap of rotten timbers, reduced to ruin by hungry woodworm and galloping damp. The single wall light, when switched on, had three degrees of brightness - dim, flicker or out. As I stood there a couple more length of jagged timber crashed onto the floor, stirring up a snowstorm of cement dust. Health and Safety rules didn't exist around here.

Looking up I saw two shadowy figures looking down at me from over the edge of the hole.

"So sorry, ducks," said one, "We didn't know anyone was using the shop yet. I say – you couldn't make us a couple of mugs of tea, could you? Strong and two sugars in each?"

I brushed myself down. "If you two want anything to eat or drink, you'd better come down and shovel this timber out the back door. I can't have such an awful mess here when there's food around."

There were two sharp intakes of breath from above.

"Well, I don't know about that," said one.

But I knew that I was holding a trump card. There is one vital word in the English language that keeps this country running and workmen working. Tea. Good, strong, hot cuppas.

"No cleared kitchen, no tea." But I threw in tempting bait. "How about some tasty fresh-baked Cornish pasties that came in this morning?"

Within seconds, the two figures, in overalls and clutching large shovels, scuttled in the front door.

"Get the kettle on, love," said the older one as they dashed past.

This was my introduction to Will and Nippy, both gifted at smelling a freshly watered teabag at a hundred yards, and calling the consumption, at one sitting, of three Cornish pasties, a hot pie, jam doughnuts and three mugs of tea each, 'a little snack.'

Will was tall and gaunt, with pale hair going thin on top. One of his eyes was scarred, he couldn't see much out of it. He said the damage was the result of an accident playing darts – someone with bad aim had gone for the wrong bull's eye. One of his little jokes. Whenever I saw him he always seemed to have a hammer in one hand and a mug in the other.

Nippy was a fresh faced, blond haired teenager with the most incredible blue eyes. Slung low around his hips was a belt holding various tools. He put me in mind of a western gunslinger; I somehow expected to find myself looking down the barrels of a couple of chisels. His nickname mystified me, I never did find out if it was attributed to his work or his love life, although judging by the number of nubile young females that, in rotation, met him after work, probably the latter.

Both of them stood looking the heap of rotten timbers, taking stock of the situation. They gave it a bit of a poke and pushed it around. Another cloud of white dust drifted into the air.

Spitting chewing gum onto the floor, Will said, "Before we get stuck in, it might be a good idea if we open the door to the back yard in readiness to shovel this mess out."

"Fine," replied Nippy, "But we have a problem, there's no key in the frigging lock."

They were far from happy at seeing their precious tea break moving even further away, so instead, tried to push open a small window beside the door. But that was jammed in its frame.

"Sodding thing," grunted Nippy, producing a hammer from his tool belt and angrily bashed away until it finally creaked open. The mouldering timbers were then poked through the aperture in double quick time.

Leaving them to it, I fled to the toilet with my knees held tightly together. That hadn't got a ceiling either. There was no toilet paper, the bowl smelt of stale urine and obviously hadn't seen a bottle of bleach for a long time. I rushed back out, checked the shop for customers, thankfully there were none, grabbed a few tissues from the dispenser on the counter and dashed back. Knickers down, I wiped the seat and sank thankfully onto it.

Out of the corner of my eye, I saw something move under the edge of the carpet. Now in full flood, I could only sit and watch as a long pair of feelers emerged from beneath the material, followed by the equally large body of a big, black cockroach. It sat in the corner, meticulously cleaning its antennae with long jointed front legs, seemingly unaware of my presence.

From my trapped position, the three cups of tea, one mug of coffee and a coke were taking a horrendously long time to filter out. When I was finally able to move, it stopped, looked up at me and scuttled under the door.

Hitching up my knickers, I followed. It was heading for an alcove in the passageway, filled with shelf fittings. But it never got there, well, not that time. I thought, "Oh, no, not cockroaches again," and catching up with it as it clattered across a patch of lino, stamped on it with all the ferocity I could muster. To my amazement it got up and carried on, although a little more slowly and probably with a horrible headache. I grabbed a wooden mallet Will had left lying on the floor, and hit it hard on its head, which did stop it in its tracks. As it lay there, I screamed, "Will, Nippy, there's a bloody big cockroach in here, please come and get it out."

Like gallant knights, they rushed to my aid, shovels in hands.

"What's the matter, ducks?" asked Will.

"Look, look, there's a ruddy big cockroach just crawled out from under the toilet carpet. I've bashed it and it's laid out on the floor.

I pointed to the spot, only to find there was nothing there except a single, hooked, black leg. I couldn't believe it.

"It was there. I hit it hard with your mallet. It could not have got up after that."

But it had. We peered into the alcove, but decided not to poke around too much, there might be more, and decided to report this matter to the owners.

As I washed my hands, Will and Nippy threw the last bits of timber out of the window.

Will said, "Put the kettle on love, my throat's like a wrestler's armpit and I'll be dying of dehydration soon. By the way, you've got your dress tucked into the back of your knickers."

Knickers. I didn't wish to be reminded that a pair of pants was, in part, responsible for this unfamiliar life I was now living

The Bakery

Come October, the sandwich bar closed down for the winter and I moved into the original bakery on the main road. After I'd dropped Jackie off at school, I turned up for work at ten to nine on the first day. Of Mr. Bellini there was no sign. The girl at the counter, who introduced herself as Annette, said she'd show me where everything was. After that I was on my own on the bread and cake counter, whilst she and the kitchen staff cooked and served the meals. I donned a striped pink pinafore and cap before having a good look around.

Annette said, "The bread comes out fresh each morning from the bakery next door and is displayed on those long glass shelves along the back. Cream cakes all go in the refrigerated unit, all the other cakes are stacked in any spaces that are left. Any extras go into that cupboard beside the bread shelves."

I noticed there were wicker baskets filled with hundreds of assorted rolls stored beneath the loaves, alongside a shiny, food-dispensing unit containing salad items, sliced meats and grated cheese. These, I was told, were for customers wanting special made up rolls.

"When you are making sandwiches or filling rolls, stuff in plenty of lettuce, its cheap, and makes them look full."

"Why don't the cakes have any price tickets on them?" I asked Annette.

"Oh, we don't bother with that," she said, "He's always altering the prices. On the cupboard door there's some sort of a price list, work off that."

I would, if I could have read it. The typed notice must have been done on an old typewriter with a past – its – sell – by - date ribbon. Worse still, the multitude of products had not been listed in a chronological or alphabetical order. Customers buying a dozen different cakes had to wait an age before I could sort out the costs. When I mentioned this to Annette, she laughed and said, "Oh, just make up prices as you go along. Most of the customers won't know the difference."

I felt this was not the right way to carry on, so in my own time at home, I carefully made a new list, putting the cakes in some kind of order. I bought it back and said to Mr. Bellini, "Please can you check that this is all correct?"

He studied it.

"Is thisa what you hava been charging the customers?"

"Well, yes."

He angrily stabbed at the list.

"Thisa is all wrong, we make no profit."

A red pen appeared from his pocket and he zapped through most of the product prices, upping them by about 20%.

"Thisa is now right."

He thrust the amended list at me.

"You get it dona right."

I soon learnt that whatever any of his constantly changing staff did, Mr. Bellini would come along and find fault with it, shouting loudly at the poor, bewildered employees, accompanied by lots of arm waving and finger jabbing. When he wasn't causing us grief in the shop, he was watching us constantly on the security cameras.

I wondered how big the file was on this business at the Job Centre, as part time staff didn't usually last more than a week, quickly departing with varying suggestions as to what he could do with, and where he could put, his cream cakes and French sticks. Annette stayed on.

"How do you put up with him?" I asked her, after he had, yet again, re-arranged all my carefully displayed cakes.

"I've been here six years," she said, "I've got used to his funny little ways, I ignore them and get on with it."

I wished I could be so easy going. Eager to please, but nervous of the next verbal attack, I tried to work around his illogical reasoning. We had to handle all the cakes with special metal tongs. When I commented that he was picking them up with his bare hands when he served the customers, his answer was, "Buta I'm the boss. Theya don't mind me touching the food."

I gave up and accepted his erratic temper and constant moving around of the cake displays. If they had to be in a certain place one week, it definitely wasn't the right place next week. And I got told off.

"But you said…" just fell on deaf ears.

"I wanna them here," he would shout at me, poking a bony digit in my face. So close did he come each time, I feared that his index finger might get parked up my left nostril and cause permanent disfigurement. He was constantly desperate to keep money flowing in and hated to lose a sale. His blood pressure went off the scale if he heard any of us say, "Sorry, we're sold out."

He grumbled if we seemed incapable of selling the huge pile of bread rolls each day, because he then had to pack the leftovers into plastic bags and put them in the deep freeze. Any enquiries after they'd been stored and he'd be rushing out to the kitchen, grabbing a few, zapping them through the microwave and then producing them with the comment, "Just coma out of the oven."

If the shop was busy and we had to do any overtime, there was never a penny extra in our wages. He argued that according to our contracts (which didn't exist), we had reached no agreement about being paid for extra time. So, unbeknown to him, we made sure we got compensation from him in other ways. One free meal each and limited amounts of tea or coffee were allowed, but because the shop was constantly busy, we all got used to grabbing a bite 'on the hoof,' eating and drinking whilst carrying on working. If you did snatch a chance to sit down it was odds on you'd be called back to serve.

However, Antonio, as I was now allowed to call him, had other businesses to supervise and employees to annoy, so he would periodically drive off from his parking spot on the double yellow lines outside, and be gone for two to three hours. I'd watch the yellow Mercedes pull away, check that it had left the area and then we'd all raid the cake and drinks cabinets.

He forgot something one day and just as we were enjoying a feast of delicious cakes, I saw his car pull up outside.

"He's back," I yelled.

We froze in horror, creamy evidence stuck around our mouths. Cake remains were hastily disposed of down the nearest cracks and crevices. Annette, who was eating in the kitchen, lost her grip in the slippery remains of a custard slice, and it splattered across the worktop.

"Oh, my God, help," she yelled.

Kitchen staff rushed to clear away the flaky crust and custard contents as Antonio stopped to chat up a female customer in the doorway. By the time he'd finished trying to charm the pants off her, we'd wiped up all the mess and were all busily finding something to do.

If he didn't go out, we found the cake cupboard useful, as, the large doors, when open, hid us from the security cameras, and it would appear to Antonio that we were sorting out cakes instead of having a quick nibble.

Occasionally, we wouldn't see him all day, and then there was a happy atmosphere. He often said he was away 'collecting relatives from Heathrow airport.'

"Members of the Mafia, more like," suggested one customer. Certainly large numbers of Italians homed in on the shop, where they'd sit for hours, chat loudly and drink endless cups of coffee. There were a few mysterious ones who glided silently in, gave Antonio a nod and then they'd all troop into his office and shut the door. It was made very clear that when that door was closed, no - one knocked, went in, or in any way, disturbed them.

"Definitely got to be the British branch of the Mafia," we joked, ready to believe this. After four or five hours they would emerge, shake hands effusively and arrange another meeting. I was in awe to be rubbing shoulders with real Mafioso. Who were they plotting to bump off next, or were they just making arrangements to visit the nearest abattoir for a fresh horse's head?

When two health inspectors turned up for a spot check, I gazed at the forbidden door and wondered if it meant instant dismissal if I knocked and got Antonio out. The large lady in the white coat was insistent; they really did have to speak to him. I could almost hear Antonio saying angrily, 'Eliz a bet, why do you do this when I tell you not to?' Oh, to hell with it. I raised a hand to knock and then noticed the door was not quite shut. I gave it a gentle push and cautiously peered in. Settled in the comfy armchairs were four little Italians, fast asleep. Playing cards and empty wine bottles were strewn across the desk. I quietly shut the door and said, "I'm afraid Mr. Bellini is engaged at the moment, can you call in another time?"

Our days were often livened up by visits from colourful characters, especially Pat and Peg Leg Pete, who were both exceedingly fond of alcohol. Pat was well into pensionable age, with a florid face, grubby raincoat and a hideous straw hat that she embellished with a weird and unusual variety of objects. Some days she might have a bit of holly or privet stuck in it, competing with a plastic windmill on a stick. Other times she's poke empty cigarette packets onto a strip of wood, which projected forward from the front of her hat like some bizarre unicorn's horn.

As Pete only had one leg, she pushed him around in a squeaky old wheelchair. They would park themselves at strategic places around the town and beg money 'for a cup of tea' from unsuspecting and sympathetic visitors, who were told he was a victim of the Falklands war. The locals were more inclined to believe the 'urban myth' alternative of the lost leg, that Pat and Pete had had one too many of their alcoholic arguments and she'd tipped him out of his wheelchair in front of an Eastbourne to Victoria train.

But they still went everywhere together, constantly shouting and arguing, always clutching a few bottles of sherry or whisky, which were downed at a speedy rate. Although they had a council flat, they preferred to live rough; constantly begging during the day and dossing down on tombstones in the churchyard or sprawled drunkenly across benches in the local park. You could always tell where they had been by the growing pile of discarded Haig and Harvey bottles.

When they'd had too much to drink, which was just about always, they could turn nasty, especially Pat. Purple faced when roused, she would help herself to things she fancied from shops and make no effort to pay for them. When challenged, she became abusive, then physically aggressive. Pete, being of a more peaceable nature, would try and grab hold of her, saying, "Now, come on, dear, that's enough." This usually produced a swift backhander from Pat that often knocked him clean out of his wheelchair.

Barred from most shops because of their outrageous behaviour, they had to rely on like-minded alcoholic acquaintances to get their booze and shopping. A few warning squeaks from that wheelchair and all the shops in the area suddenly locked their doors and put up 'gone to lunch" notices.

We could hear them having one of their usual noisy exchanges, this time in the middle of the busy main road. This came to a climax when Pat parked Pete in his wheelchair amongst the traffic and left him there. Unable to turn to free the brake, he couldn't move away, so he just sat and shouted obscenities at the angry, hooting drivers. Shrieking like a banshee and waving a bottle of sherry in the air, Pat wove an unsteady path into the shop.

My heart sank. Her face, as usual, was crimson, a good barometer of the high amount of drink inside her. The hat sported two little upright sticks with a length of silver tinsel strung between them. You had to hand it to her; she never wore the same design twice. As she barged in, waiting customers stepped warily back, looking to see what action I was going to take. Not a lot, if I could help it, just try and get rid of her as quickly as possible. I didn't want to be washing sherry out of my hair or picking bits of glass out of my bruised scalp. In her present mood, any problem, however minor, could catapult her into trying to smash up the glass cabinets or kick the café tables over.

With far from clean hands, she selected a chiabatta loaf from the display basket on the counter and held it aloft for Pete to see. A kindly soul had let off the brake and wheeled him to the doorway, where he was now picking his teeth with a bit of stick.

"Want one these, ducks?"

"No, I don't want that foreign rubbish," he yelled back, moving on with his orifice excavations and began poking up his nose with a dirt engrained fingernail. One or two customers slid out of the door, deftly dodging Pat's flailing arms. She sifted through various loaves, waving them at him to attract his attention. But he'd lost interest and was trying to extract some coins from passers-by. With his hand held out he kept on muttering, "Thank you sir, thank you, madam," in anticipation of financial reward that would be quickly spent on booze.

All he got was a large bloomer loaf banged down on the top of his head, as Pat exploded, "Listen to me when I'm talking to you." The wheelchair squeaked loudly, wobbled slightly at the onslaught and Pete's mouth turned down at the corners of his leathery face.

"Bugger off, you old bat," he yelled at Pat, but she was engrossed in changing her weapons of war, substituting the bloomer for a large farmhouse loaf. As she held it aloft, Antonio, having witnessed what was happening on the security cameras, shot out of his office. Gesticulating furiously, he pulled up in front of Pat.

"Whata do you think you are doing? Puta that down at once."

Still clutching the loaf, she halted in her tracks. Pete hastily propelled himself out of sight, away from these signs of a massive, erupting storm. Antonio snatched the loaf back.

"Donna you dare do these things with my food. Go away." He glared at Pat, whose face was now glowing red with fury. She didn't often get spoken to in such a manner. Most shopkeepers, eager to be rid of her, would just turn a blind eye and let her get away with whatever she fancied. In all of her days of skulduggery on the streets, no-one had ever spoken to her like this. She stood facing Antonio and boiled. She'd met her match, and was rendered speechless.

Still flapping his arms about, Antonio, oblivious to a fascinated audience, carried on.

"Geta out, geta out, otherwise I kicka your arse all down the road."

The stuffing was completely knocked out of Pat and, with her silver tinsel trembling, her eyeballs bulging, she backed away from her bristling opponent. In a final act of defiance she poured the last drops of sherry onto the floor and smashed the bottle on the doorstep as she left. Pete got another whack round the head, but played to her strengths by producing a whisky bottle from the depths of his filthy raincoat. A couple of swigs each and they noisily careered away down the road, scattering unwary pedestrians.

After clearing up the mess, serving the remaining customers and seeing Antonio off to one of his other shops, I swapped places with Annette and went to work in the kitchen. On the preparation table were a dozen cooked chickens, laid out in indecent posture, on their backs, with legs wide apart. It reminded me of my non-existent love life since the departure of Everard and his well filled trousers. Apart from a couple of dodgy handshakes from leering husbands and a grope from an over -friendly male customer, there had been nothing out there for me. I needed to look a bit harder.

But this day of problems wasn't yet over. As we freshened up the counter display, a plump blue-bottle, big as a ripe blackberry, but obviously with dodgy eyesight, did a couple of noisy circuits over the salad bar and belly flopped into the mayonnaise dish. The moment it surfaced and started doing a noisy, six-legged doggy paddle in the greasy fluid, the two environmental health inspectors returned for a spot check. The words 'shit' and 'fan' sprung to mind as I nudged Annette.

The fly slowly hauled itself onto the rim of the dish, squatted for a few seconds to wipe it face clean, before making an ill-judged decision to take off. But weighed down with gunge, it pitched into the adjacent coleslaw pot and started a re-run of its noisy routine.

With the two talismans of officialdom – a clipboard at the ready and a smarmy smile, the mountainous and formidable looking lady did the introductions.

"We're environmental health officers and we have come back to do an inspection of the property. I'm Ms Maitland and this is Mr. Ferdinand."

She pushed forward a little man with thick-rimmed glasses, who seemed intent on studying the floor. He visibly winced as she snapped on her rubber gloves with a vicious twang. Donning a white hat that perched perilously on the top of her pepper and salt bouffant hair, and hitching her overall around her ample bosom, she said, "Right, where shall we start?"

"Oh God," muttered Annette, "What are we going to do." I could see both of us being out of our jobs by tonight, as Antonio would blame us if there were any nasty problems, like large flies in the food.

The blue bottle came up for air with another noisy buzzing session. Annette suddenly developed a hacking cough as she hastily shifted the salad bowls around and gave the insect a discreet whack with the tongs. It sank beneath the surface.

Forcing what I hoped was a pleasant grin, I said, "The boss isn't around at the moment, perhaps another day might be suitable. We're only counter staff, so we really can't take the responsibility."

Although somewhat thwarted for the second time, Ms. Maitland couldn't resist doing a radar style sweep of the shop. I guess she was hoping to spot some dreadful hygiene mistakes before she departed, thus scoring a few brownie points on her clipboard and justifying the visit. As she turned away the spluttering fly re-appeared; I seized the opportunity to throw a large dollop of coleslaw over it.

"Oh well," she said, removing her hat, gloves and overall, "We'll come back another time." With little man in tow, she flounced out.

"Thank goodness for that," sighed Annette as we tipped the coleslaw and now deceased fly into the bin. "This has been quite a day."

We then heard a loud voice from the other side of the counter,

"Wot, no rolls?"

Turning around we saw a bleached blonde in a floral frock, who was probably seeing 21 for the third time around, standing there hands on hips, with a disgruntled look on her leathery brown face.

Annette gave her one of her forced smiles.

"Well, we are usually sold out by this time of the day."

"Well, this is not good enough. I'm going to Butlins tomorrow. Are you sure you haven't any rolls left? That little man always finds some for me from outside."

She leaned over the counter, trying to peer into the kitchen.

"He's not here, and we definitely haven't got any rolls left over."

"Got a bloomer loaf then, I'll make up something with that?"

"No, we've sold out of bread as well."

"Well, what am I going to take to Butlins? I suppose I'll have to go to that bakery up the road. They only sell uncut bread. If I bring it down to you, can you put it through your slicing machine?"

"Sorry, can't do that for you," said Annette, as she deliberately started to take the slicing machine to pieces and began washing the parts in hot, soapy water. "We have to clean it each day at this time."

Bleached blonde took the hint and went.

"What we have to put up with" said Annette, furiously digging bits of crust out of awkward corners of the machine. I could only agree.

Comforted by the regular weekly wage packet, I stuck at the job for a year. But when I said I wanted to take a week's paid holiday, as had been agreed, Antonio promptly upped the ante and said part-time staff now had to work for two years before they got paid holidays.

"I'm not stopping here much longer," I said angrily to Annette, "There must be another job out there I can do without all this hassle."

The catalyst occurred a couple of week's later, when I must have been suffering from menopausal PMT and was decidedly tetchy. It was a hot summer's day; the chill cabinets were working like fury to keep the cream cakes cold, and blowing a stream of expelled hot air on me. Hot flushes in stereo. Serving a long queue of impatient Saturday customers on my own, as staff had again left, I could feel a torrent of sweat flowing down my back. Even the ceiling fans offered no coolness.

Antonio emerged from his office, head down, shoulders squared up, I could see he was definitely looking for trouble. After a busy morning, the cakes were now in a muddle and I'd had no chance to tidy up. I knew he'd go on at me about it, all delivered in a loud voice in front of everyone. The back of my neck prickled. This was High Noon time.

He stopped.

"Eliz a bet, why are there no bags on da hooks for da cakes?"

I carried on with what I was doing, and carefully explained, "I've been extremely busy and I haven't had the time. I'll do it in a minute."

He snapped into Hitler mode, threw his arms about a lot and got red in the face.

"Do it now."

This was it. Head to head and lose my job time. I wasn't backing down now. I squared up to him and very deliberately said, "Read my lips. I'll do it when I'm ready."

He came up close. Being small, his eyeballs were about level with my cleavage.

"Eliz a bet, I donna like the way you talk to me."

Now wound up enough to be in a fighting mood I bent over, the answer punching to get out from behind my teeth.

"And I don't like the way you talk to me."

A hush descended, everyone in the café was listening to this verbal tennis match as it reached 3-3.

Antonio drew himself up to his full 4ft 10 inches and spluttered, "If a you don't like the job, there's the door."

I tore off the pinafore and hat and angrily thrust them into his hands. The impact caused his huge glasses to drop off the end of his nose. They crashed to the floor and broke. Feeling spiteful, I wanted to stamp all over the shattered pieces but resorted to vicious verbals instead.

"You're a bloody lousy boss and you treat your staff appallingly. I certainly don't want to work for you any more."

A collective snigger rippled amongst the customers. Antonio stood there, open mouthed, completely lost for words. It was game, set and match to me as I marched out, head held high. But I hadn't got a job, again. And now was definitely not the time to ask for a reference.

Making Do

"Oh mum, you're embarrassing me again," muttered Jackie, as she slunk lower into the depths of the car.

"Well, we've got to make do," I replied, rummaging amongst the contents of a well filled skip. Back on benefits, money was tight. But this was now an age of 'Don't move, improve.' The local area was filling up with cavernous bright yellow or orange metal containers filled high with inviting, discarded items.

Their presence had turned me into an impulsive skip maniac, I couldn't drive past any skips that were filled with rejected goodies, I had to stop and have a poke around. Other peoples' unwanted bits were my prize trophies to be carted home 'to do something with,' and they all cost nothing. So Jackie might have been a bit late for school, but, from the detritus of a household clear out, I'd been able to uplift a complete front door finished in white gloss paint, with brass handles and hinges. There was enough electrical cable to add some extra sockets in the house and the four elegant table legs would make perfect supports for runner beans I was trying to grow. On the way back home, I added an upright vacuum cleaner that had been dumped on the top of a load of rubbish. Although missing a locking device that kept it upright when stationery, it worked, and replaced my old cylindrical one that a few days previously had died with a loud bang and a cloud of smoke.

The best prizes were a floral three-piece cottage suite, missing one wheel, plus a white patio table with three grubby chairs which could easily be scrubbed clean. After knocking on the owner's door and asking if I could take it all away, I had the problem of getting it home, as my estate car was nowhere near big enough. A kind and helpful neighbour offered to do the collecting, but it turned out he owned just a tiny trailer towed by a mini. The armchairs fitted neatly into the trailer, and rather than make two journeys, we tied the sofa onto his ancient roof rack. This turned out to be a perilously rocky affair when the mini started to move. Jackie and I, with the patio set, followed at a careful distance, watching the sofa bouncing around and hoping nothing would end up in the road.

Looking in my rear view mirror I said to Jackie, "Oh, no, there's a police car that's pulled out of a side turning and nudged in behind me." She slid down in her seat. I felt prickles go up the back of my neck as I saw that the sofa, held on by bits of string and rope, had started to slip. Its weight made the mini's steering somewhat unstable and the car began to waver around. At that point the blue light and sirens came on. "Oh shit," I muttered, foreseeing all of us being hauled into court and fined horrible amounts for carrying an unstable load.

But to our relief, the police car was after greater prey as it roared past, chasing a motorist doing double the speed limit.

"Thank God for that," said the neighbour when we arrived home, "I thought we were a goner, I've just noticed my tax disc is out of date."

The suite fitted in a treat with a couple of books shoved underneath the wheel-less end to stop it rocking and the two deck chairs we had been sitting on went out in the garden, to be joined by the scrubbed clean patio set.

Having furnished and carpeted most of the house with re-cycled items, and adding a working lawn mower to the growing amount of collectables in the shed, I felt rather proud of my efforts until Jackie wistfully said, "Wouldn't it be lovely if we could have a conservatory, where we could sit out there and enjoy ourselves?"

"Yes, I agree, but you don't find those sitting in skips on a daily basis. All I can afford at the moment are two sheets of greenhouse glass mounted on a quartet of bamboo canes. We'll think about it when I get another job."

And this is where Roger became 'our knight in shining armour.' Rog was everybody's friend. He knew how to cook the most fantastic recipes to feed two or twenty-two, could turn his hand to any building challenge, from adding an extension to garden design, and re-wire a whole house in his lunch time. He was a brilliant member of many pub quiz teams, he knew most of the answers and he loved all things archaeological, especially fossils. His age was unknown, his baby face as unlined, but his wheat coloured hair was teased over an ever-increasing bald patch.

But Rog had an Achilles' heel; he couldn't settle down to a conventional way of life. Most of the time he lived in a rust - bucket of a car, which was hardly ever taxed or insured. If he was renovating a house, which was quite often, he would move in and camp there for the duration. When the job was finished, he'd simply move on. All the local cafes, bistros and restaurants were well acquainted with Rog; he'd turn up, cook himself a meal and pay for it by washing up, cleaning or doing repairs. It was a kind of bartering system, which all those who knew Rog were happy with, because he always gave one hundred and ten percent in return. Occasionally he'd disappear for months, and rumour had it that he had nipped over to Holland to avoid the tax man, cash in hand being the name of his game. Then he'd suddenly re-appear and there was always a stack of jobs waiting for him around town.

We met him as we shopped for baked beans in the local superstore.

"How are you doing, Rog?" I asked, as I looked for any cut price bargains.

"Fine, I've just been renovating the interior of an old

paddle steamer," he replied.

"Wow, I bet that was interesting."

"Yes, there's not many of them left now, but this one should be good for a few years. It's sailing up to Scotland shortly, going to be used for the tourist trade."

We sat and had a cup of coffee, catching up on the gossip and local news.

"What are you doing now?" he asked.

"Not a lot, I've just lost my job. I'm looking for another one, but I can spend a bit more time with Jackie. She's got this idea that because I was earning a reasonable wage, we could afford to have a conservatory added onto the house. All her friends seem to have one."

"I'll do it for you, if you'll feed me," offered Rog.

"You wouldn't want my mummy cooking for you," chipped in Jackie, "She's the only person I know that can get boiled eggs to explode out of the saucepan and stick to the ceiling. She can even burn salads."

"Oh stop it, I'm not that bad," I had to reply, "But would you really do this. I couldn't afford to pay you much and the materials would be priced completely out of my pocket."

"No, no, I can get most of the materials for nothing."

"Are you sure? Well, I've got a nice back door with brass furniture that might get us started."

"Yep, I've nothing on for a few days; if we can get all the bits together I can put it up in next to no time. I know where we can get some abandoned timber for the corners and plastic corrugated sheeting for the roof, although we'll have to collect them in your estate car, mine is too small. We will have to look around for some bricks for the base wall and I've got a bit of cement left over from my last job."

"Oh Rog you're an angel, I never thought we'd be able to do this."

Having said our goodbyes we got into our car.

"Hey look, mum," cried Jackie, "Bricks."

And sure enough, in the opposite row of the car park was a builder's van, filled with used bricks. The back doors were open and sat inside were two bronzed and tough looking men drinking tea out of polystyrene cups.

I couldn't turn down an opportunity like this.

"Guys, have you any plans for those bricks?"

"Taking them down to the tip in a mo, missus," said one, "We're dumping them."

"Well, if you want to transfer them from your van to my car, I'll save you a trip. They're just perfect for my needs."

Two more cups of tea and a couple of Chelsea buns bought us a generous amount of re-usable bricks. The car's suspension was far from happy with the added weight, but we spent an industrious evening cleaning the bricks, leaving a good pile for Rog to get started with. In no time at all he'd got a low wall cemented in and Jackie became excited at the prospect of showing off the conservatory to her friends.

Rog stoically ate my pathetic offerings of burnt sausages, bacon fried to a crisp, which shattered as soon as he stuck a fork in it, and teeth-breaking crunchy chips. He passed on the adhesive yellow globules that were meant to be fried eggs when Jackie remarked, "Mum, you'd better tell him what's on that plate, in case he has to describe it to the doctor." Instead he expressed more pleasure in a continuing supply of tea and coffee backed up by mountainous ham and salad sandwiches.

In spite of the hiccups in my cookery department, Rog soldiered on.

"We need to use your car again today," he said, as the work progressed upwards. "I know someone who's changing their double glazed windows and there's a local pub that's having a new roof on their conservatory. The plastic sheets they've taken off are pretty good and they just want to get rid of them."

We ran a shuttle service, collecting up all the materials. The door I'd dragged out of a skip was fitted in and soon there was just the roof that needed putting on. We were so near.

Then Rog failed to turn up. We waited for days before asking around, but no one knew where he was. Eventually word reached us that he'd done one of his disappearing acts again and gone to ground in Holland to avoid the tax man.

With winter approaching, we were left with a superbly erected, but roofless conservatory and a distraught Jackie who insisted, "You drove him away with your dreadful cooking."

Dog Sitting

I went to visit friend Sadie, who had also lost her job. Over a glass of cheap plonk, she said, "I've an idea about raising some extra money. Our kids are growing up fast and they're constantly in need of new clothes or shoes, there are school trips to pay for, and knackered appliances in both our homes regularly stop working, or fall apart. How about if we advertise a dog and pet sitting service? You know, live in people's homes and look after their pets whilst they are on holiday." That seemed a terrific idea. No outlay, bed and board provided, and getting paid as well. We decided to give it a go and scratched up enough money between us to put a small advertisement in the local free-Ad.

The day the paper appeared, I hovered hopefully around the phone. It didn't ring. My washing machine made some weird gurgling noises and piddled on the floor. Cursing its timing, I hauled out the dripping clothes, did a hand wash and hung them on the washing line. It promptly snapped under the weight. I threw the soiled clothes into the laundry basket and kicked it under the table.

"But I won't have any clean knickers for school tomorrow," wailed Jackie.

"Tough," I said, through gritted teeth, "You'll have to turn the pair you're wearing inside out and like it."

Then the phone rang. Shrill, loud and demanding. I pounced.

"The Wright pet sitting service, may I help you?" I enquired politely, trying to appear totally professional. A pause, then a woman spoke.

"I understand you do dog sitting?" Her voice had the crisp diction of a BBC newsreader with class. I felt elated. Our very first customer and posh with it.

"Yes, we do," I replied. Mrs. Two-plums-in-the-mouth went on.

"My husband and I are going away for a long weekend. We have five dogs that will cost us a small fortune in kennel fees. It's going to be more economic to have someone to live in for a few days. Would you be interested?"

Would we just.

"When would it be for?" I enquired, trying hard to keep up the best telephone voice.

"Next weekend."

"If you'll hold the line a minute, I'll consult my diary."

We hadn't got around to buying one, so having put down the phone, I noisily rustled a few sheets of paper and counted to ten.

"Yes, I think we can fit you in. Would you like me to come over and discuss arrangements?"

The address was in the local area known as Manor Trees. Very select, where you were looked down on if you drove anything less than a top of the range car and had a 4x4 as backup. I could already see the washing machine back in action.

I drove over to Sadie's house, where she was doing her bit for the environment by de-fleaing her cats using a steel nit comb and a pot of hot water instead of a spray can full of chemicals.

"Good news, we've got our first job, dog sitting in the poshest area of town, Manor Trees. That's a real moneyed area."

We couldn't believe our luck. As the layer of fleas learning to do the breast stroke in the pot of water grew, so did our redefined and totally over the top visions of life on the posh side of the railway lines. We could soon be sipping Martinis beside their swimming pool, (they'd be bound to have a pool) and walk barefoot on luxurious Chinese carpets. Their American sized freezers would be overflowing with exotic foods, so we could enjoy the delights of best rump steak, caviar and salmon. For a few brief days we could be living in the sort of luxury we could only dream about. Dare I begin to feel happy? Could I let my spirits lift so I need not worry so much about our poor financial situation?

"You go and keep the appointment," said Sadie, "I'll collect the kids from school."

So I made my way to Manor Trees, wide as the M4 and lined with imposing houses. Each had immaculately tended lawns sliced by gravel driveways leading up to double, even triple, garages. There was not a discarded crisp packet in sight, no holes in the cedar wood fences, any boarded-up windows, graffiti, or traffic cones stuck rakishly on top of gateposts.

I pulled into the side of the road to look at the numbers. I wanted forty-two. As the car engine idled, the gearbox began to make its usual clanking noise, which grated into the pristine silence. Embarrassed, I switched off the engine. Perhaps I'd better not appear in this old heap, it might tend to mar that professional image I was so keen to promote. I walked along looking for the right number, but most of the properties had names such as Cherry Trees or Chestnuts delicately painted in swirls of floral lettering on ceramic discs fixed on their gate posts.

Further along, the road began to take on a more countrified appearance. The houses became bungalows the size of Canadian ranches. The odd daisy had even got a foothold here. Counting the numbers, I came almost to the end of the road before it turned the corner and blended into Magnolia Walk. There was no sign of any more buildings, just an unruly green, thick, high hedge that had obviously run rampant for many years. Threaded through the middle were spiky blackberry branches, their frayed, woody stems sticking out ready to scratch unwary passers - by. A froth of cream honeysuckle had knitted and purled itself into the foliage. This bit of land looked as if it was an unresolved, technical hiccup in the local planning department.

Had we been the victims of a practical joke? I felt a deep ache settle in my stomach, we'd wanted this job so much, and now it seemed there was nothing. I sighed, and thought, 'Oh well, its back to beans and baked potatoes.'

I glanced at a gap in the hedge where a few bits of wood held together with string seemed to be trying to pass as a gate. Scratched into the decaying timbers were the figures 42.

Curious, but cautious, I squeezed through the space and was confronted by a wilderness of a garden that could have been Sussex's answer to the Amazon rain forest. The trees and weeds were so high the sun had given up the struggle to reach the dank, smelly, muddy ground. Spilling out of a couple of torn bin bags lying just inside, were rusty Pedigree Chum tins, crumpled newspapers, plastic cartons and whisky bottles. A can clattered and rolled away as a large grey rat, in panic mode, scampered into the undergrowth, ropey tail held high. I gasped and stepped back - what a tip.

A narrow green path wove its way through the tangled mass of vegetation. Common sense said, 'Let's forget this and go home.' But we really did need the money, and for all I knew, they might be eccentric millionaires.

'At least go and have a look,' I muttered to myself. The sound of barking dogs spurred me on. The gloomy, green tunnel reluctantly opened up into a clearing. Before me stood a house that defied the logistics of structural engineering. A desperate estate agent might have advertised it as 'a house full of character;' an even more desperate agent could have said, 'a challenge for DIY enthusiasts -preferably owning a bulldozer.' The building had a distinct list to starboard with a jigsaw puzzle of large cracks zigzagging down the brickwork at the front. A TV aerial hung drunkenly from the chimney-pot.

'Go home,' said the warning voice in my head, as the eccentric millionaire idea evaporated, but - something drew me on. At least the ragged grass at the front had been cut, probably with a pair of scissors. Capability Brown it was not. Bits of broken paving slabs edged in purple aubrietia led up to a small front porch. Long ago, probably in the last war, the door had been bright blue, now it was faded and peeling.

As I lifted my hand to knock, I could feel my heart thumping painfully in my chest. What had I let myself in for? I took a deep breath and rapped loudly, which set the dogs barking again. No one answered, so I rapped again, a little harder. The barking went up two decibels. Then the handle rattled. I fixed my mouth into what I hoped was a pleasant smile and waited. A couple of bolts grated back and the handle rattled again. The door moved a centimetre inwards and stuck.

"Oh, bugger," intoned a deep voice as its owner tugged away. With a creak and a groan the door slowly opened to reveal a refugee from the Adam's family, Lurch's twin brother, all 6ft 4inches of him. He leaned over me.

"Y-e-e-e—s?" he enquired in a gravely voice.

I was rooted to the spot by this weird sample of masculinity. Wild, unkempt hair, a face distinctly in need of a shave, dirt streaked cardigan over a grubby shirt, tight fitting black trousers with a circle of dusty markings around a partially done-up zip, and a pair of tweed slippers that were split at the front revealing dirt ingrained toenails.

"Y-e-e-e-s?" he enquired again.

The friendly smile was still stuck on my face, horror had paralysed my muscles.

"Are you Mr. Carter-Patterson?" I enquired without the assistance of moving lips. A ventriloquist would have been proud of the attempt.

"Y-e-e-e-e-s," replied Lurch 2.

This was getting ridiculous. My brain finally jumped into some kind of pathetic action.

"Mrs C-C-Carter-P-P-Patterson phoned me about doing some dog sitting, is she here?"

"No."

Lurch 2 scratched his head and a snowstorm of dandruff flew into the air. He carefully scrutinised the hand that had done the scalp scratching and began to pick out bits from his fingernails.

"She's out, be back in a minute. You'd better come in and look at the dogs."

Not wishing to appear rude, but poised to run, I followed him inside. There was a pungent aroma in the air, a mixture of smelly dog and overflowing cess pit. I tried not to gag. He opened the door to a room on our left and we squelched onto a damp carpet where dog hairs had stitched themselves into the patchy pile. Frayed net curtains, held up by string, hung in the windows. Rather unnecessary, as the panes were so dirty you couldn't see in or out. The walls might have been magnolia colour originally, but over the years had turned a dirty grey. Some dubious brown dollops were stuck along the skirting board. A single, bare light bulb illuminated a host of cobwebs; the ones strung across the corners could have doubled up as hammocks. A couple of fleas jumped onto my leg.

Sitting on a ramshackle settee were three scruffy dogs bearing a passing resemblance to Beagles.

"There they be," said Lurch 2, with a hint of pride in his voice, "Our dogs. They've all got classy pedigrees, good enough to show at Crufts, any day."

The three animals uncurled themselves and slowly slid to the floor. Elderly, bony, with rheumy eyes, they shuffled towards us.

"There be our Bess, she be the best of the lot."

He pointed to the biggest dog that was limping along behind the other two. She had difficulty keeping up because one back leg wasn't working properly. It was covered in festering sores and as she carefully dragged herself across the room, little spots of blood were left on the carpet. With a loud grunt of relief she sat down by my feet and a few more fleas joined the two already into their second course on my leg.

"The missus wants to go on holiday," Lurch 2 intoned, "But I'm not sure about it. I don't want ter go."

He scratched his crotch; I just prayed he didn't go dandruff hunting in this area as the zip slipped a bit lower.

"She gets these ideas," he went on, warming to the theme, "She wants one of those, you know, lovey-dovey weekends. I don't want any of that stuff."

The idea of anyone, especially Mrs. Two-plums-in-the-mouth Carter-Patterson, having any of that stuff with Lurch 2 beggared belief. What on earth did she see in him?

An eruption of furious barking from outside broke up the conversation. Lurch 2 shot upright and turned towards the open patio doors leading out to the back garden. I caught a glimpse of a wire run, inside which two large, black shapes were hurling themselves back and forth, plainly intent on murdering a swiftly passing ginger cat. With a wild screech, Lurch 2 grabbed a newspaper lying on the table, folded it into a tube, and, angrily jabbering away in some strange foreign language, ran down the garden path. In top gear action, his long legs didn't quite co-ordinate with the rest of his body. He reminded me of a dysfunctional clown on stilts. He began bashing away with the newspaper at the rusty and holey wire netting, which made the dogs snarl and bark even more. As they jumped up, with teeth bared, his head appeared to be in imminent danger of being ripped off. Eventually he gave up the jabbering and banging and moved away. The dogs quietened down and slunk into a rickety wooden structure, which appeared to serve as a kennel.

"Got to show 'em whose boss," he said, tossing the tattered remnants of the Sun back on the table.

"Them's show dogs too, Austrian hunting hounds. Have to talk to them in their own language, they don't understand otherwise."

He gave his trousers a hitch; the zip gave up the struggle and slid right down. I sidled to the patio entrance ready to make my escape. In an emergency dash, I didn't want a tug-of-war with the porch door. Lurch 2 came close.

"How did you get here, by car?"

I nodded, edging away.

"What you got then?"

"An Ital estate, I mumbled, feeling my other leg being attacked by more hungry fleas.

"I've got one of those, lovely cars, aren't they?"

A whiff of whisky was blown into my nostrils, accentuated by a nasty smell wafting out from behind the settee. Bess limped out, her jaws hitched into a satisfied smile. The two other dogs nipped behind to investigate.

"Would you like to see mine?" he asked.

I didn't stop to find out what he was offering to show me. I fled into the garden, saying that I'd wait for his wife to get in touch, but I was awfully busy.

I phoned Sadie when I got home – "Forget the pet sitting, I'm trying to get a family of fleas out of my car, shit off my shoes and I need a clean pair of knickers."

The Hook

"Mum," said Jackie, from somewhere within the bombsite of her bedroom, "Can I have a proper hook on the back of my door to hang my dressing-gown on?"

Having recovered from the shock of finding out that she wanted to hang something up, an action far removed from the norm, as her carpet was the usual depository for most things in her bedroom, I agreed this might be a good idea.

In the past we had used sticky backed hooks, which regularly unstuck, fell glue side down and welded themselves into the carpet. Perhaps it was now time to upgrade. I knew that somewhere in the house we had a smart chrome hook gleaned from one of my skip searches. We hunted in cupboards, bags and boxes before tracking it down in the bottom of the toolbox.

Knowing this job was going to be more advanced than simply hammering a big nail into timber, we asked the local DIY shop for advice on fitting hooks into hollow internal doors.

"You'll need some of these plugs to help hold the screws firmly in," said the assistant, passing over a small plastic box containing what looked like six dried, green caterpillars.

Back home, we laid out one hook and six plugs – but one essential item was missing - screws. But another thorough rummage in the old tin toolbox produced a couple that fitted perfectly into the two holes in the hook.

Knowing that I didn't have a good eye for straight lines, Jackie got out her school ruler, and, standing on a chair, carefully measured up for a central location. Then she made sure the hook was straight before marking the woodwork where it needed to be drilled.

Then we had another little hiccup. We didn't possess

a drill, at least, not one of those cordless types that could fast-track neat holes in the blink of an eyelid. And this job was going to need more than a pointed meat skewer thumped with a heavy hammer.

As a manless household, the best the tool box could offer was an antiquated, hand operated device, of a type that Noah might have used to construct the Ark. But it did have a drill bit about the right size, so we decided to go for it.

"We need some sticking plaster," I said.

"You're a pessimist," replied Jackie, "We're not going to cut ourselves."

"No, stick it over the place where you want to put the holes and the drill won't slip. I saw that handy hint on television the other day."

But the plaster refused to stick to the door, so Jackie, edging into know-it-all teenager, balanced on the chair and began turning the drill handle. Ten seconds later there were two neat holes in the door panel, all ready for the little green plugs.

After a couple of forceful pushes, the first one slid in, but the second green caterpillar was having none of it, clinging to the outside of the hole, before falling to pieces when we applied some persuasive pressure. So did the third and fourth. We looked at the remaining two with some trepidation, before I climbed on the chair and hit number five with a hammer. It shot right through the hole and disappeared down into the hollow cavity.

We reviewed the situation. Only one plug left. But number five had cleared a pathway, so number six went in perfectly, as did the screws.

On a jubilant high, Jackie jumped around the room, waving her arms about, yelling, "We've done it."

We stood back and admired our handiwork, which had taken over an hour to fix. The dressing-gown was ceremoniously hung in place. 'Changing Rooms eat your heart out', I thought as I shut her bedroom door, and dried green caterpillar number five rattled around inside the wood.

The Allotment

"You're the lucky one," said Sadie, "Managing to bag two part time jobs in one day, and having a cheap holiday in Spain. Your financial situation must be improving. I see a local builder has put a roof on your conservatory. Aren't you pleased with yourself?"

I had to admit I was feeling somewhat smug; employment got harder when you were coming up to pensionable age and now I'd really got a break, two actually.

"Yes, I'm working in a sandwich bar in the mornings and in a DIY shop in the afternoons. I must have heard all the variations from cheeky male customers about them 'needing a screw,' and placating poor, naïve apprentices, who've been sent along to fetch fallopian tubes from the lighting department and left handed screwdrivers from the tool section. Those that should know better have asked for striped paint, sparks for grindstones, and long weights. One youngster said did we stock sky hooks, so we sent him back to ask his superior what colour was required, cloudy blue or fluffy white."

"Liz, as you are so well occupied, I don't know whether you're interested in making any more money?"

"I'll never say 'no' to any extra income, what had you got in mind?"

"Well, dad lives just around the corner from you and he's got a small plot of land which he once used as an allotment. We could cut down on our shopping bills by growing our own food there. Think of it, delicious tomatoes, runner beans, strawberries, peas, cabbages, all fresh picked, such healthy eating. All we've got to do is dig little holes, pop in young plants, fill in the holes, water occasionally and something good is bound to come up."

We went and had a look at this patch of land. Unworked

for some years, it was just deep furrows covered in grass and rubbish. A leaning heap of rotting wood at the far end was all that remained of a shed. As we stood there in the bleakness of a January afternoon, in temperatures cold enough to stick a dog to a lamppost, it was hard to visualise how we might be able to transform this ground into a productive, fertile area. It was going to be a Herculean task. Stamping on the frozen earth and being pelted with sleet took some of the gloss off our money-making idea.

"Shall we have a proper look again in the early spring?" suggested Sadie.

"In the meantime we'd better have a stock take on any gardening tools we possess," I replied.

Not a lot, as it turned out. One hoe, one spade with a cracked handle, a pair of grass clippers with blades that got bent when I'd used them to dig out a large weed in my front lawn, and a rake with a prong missing. Poking around in the debris of the collapsing shed we found a few assorted seed trays and half a bag of compost that looked usable, after we had ditched the creepy crawlies in residence.

Some of the Sunday newspaper supplements were giving away packets of vegetable and flower seeds to readers, so we scrounged as many packets as we could from those friends and neighbours who weren't interested in horticultural propagation. We could always grow some bedding plants to sell in the late spring; in garden centres they appeared to be a real money spinner.

We got out the plastic trays, filled them with compost, after turfing out a bit more livestock that had surfaced. In my kitchen, on sheets of newspaper, we opened the packets, sprinkling on the seeds, and stacked the trays in my front room. Then we waited.

And watered, and waited. It seemed an age before one brave tomato plant poked up its tiny head. We celebrated with a bottle cheap wine. Our first baby had been born.

Within a few days, green tomato shoots were poking through in more of the trays. As the room was lit by one large picture window, they all leaned towards the light. To correct their curvatures, I turned the trays around. They bent the other way and ended up with 'S' shaped stems.

When they got big enough, we decided it was time to put each tomato plant in its own pot. A further rummage in the rubble of the shed had yielded a varying assortment of plastic pots. Some were cracked, but were adequately patched up with bandages of brown parcel tape. We teased out the baby plants from their warm, comfortable trays and potted them up, setting them out along the window sills. But they didn't like being separated from each other, after a few days most slumped sideways and appeared to be badly in need of a horticultural life support system. A few survived but in the mass re-shuffle we got the labels mixed up and couldn't tell the difference between our Minibelles and Moneymakers. So we eventually dug a few holes in a cleared patch of the allotment, shoved them in and hoped.

And they started to grow. One warm weekend afternoon, as we tended the plants we became aware that our vigorous actions had attracted a spectator. Draped over the gate, he was staring long and hard at our tomato plants. Underneath the flat, cloth cap a brain was getting into gear.

"Hey, missus, you want to pull all those spare leaves off them tomato plants."

He pointed to the lush vegetation finally going up the sticks.

"Those bits coming out the forks, snap 'em off, they're draining the plants. You won't get such a good crop if you leave them on."

His weather-browned face and pale blue eyes had an outdoor look; he was probably used to gazing across rural vistas and telling inexperienced folk what to do with their plants.

"Here, I'll do it for you."

He rolled up his sleeves, kicked open the gate with his size eleven hob nailed boots and strode across to the quivering plants. Right behind his left boot, as if attached to it, was a perky black and white Jack Russell terrier, its little short legs moving like some mechanical toy.

We watched in horror as our precious tomato plants were stripped of most of their leaves, culminating with their heads being snapped off.

"Mustn't let them have more than three trusses, otherwise all the fruit will be small." We didn't know what trusses were, but beheaded, our tomato crop was now going to be far below our truss expectations.

"Do you want any help with other plants," he enquired.

"No, no, we're fine, just a glitch in our knowledge," we hastily reassured him.

Let loose in our allotment on a regular basis, and he'd be decimating the plants faster than we could plant them.

"I'll give you a look in occasionally, see you're all right. Come on then, Jack."

He clumped up the path, followed by the dog, which detached itself from his boot just long enough lift its leg on the runner beans. I didn't fancy them any more.

As the weather got warmer, we set about trying to sort out the rest of the ground. The nettles and weeds had sprung up everywhere and brambles were taking over. I hammered out the bent grass clipper blades so they were a bit straighter, and, having no secateurs, attacked the thorny branches. One snip in four was successful. The spade with its dodgy handle finally snapped. Sadie fluttered her eyelashes at one of the male neighbours and managed to borrow a heavy man sized one. Sadly, its owner declined to help with the digging. Our wrists ached with our efforts, but we kept telling each other it would all be worth it.

The friendly owner of a local flower nursery, charmed by Sadie's well mascara'd eyelashes, big smile and low cut dress, didn't mind us sifting through his heap of reject plants. "They're only going to end up being burnt," he told us. We found some sorry looking strawberry plants and a few bedding lettuce, both of which perked up after some TLC.

The strawberries threw out a shower of white flowers, promising rich, red fruit. They would be a touch of luxury in our boring diets. We yearned for the fruits to ripen, so we could enjoy the luscious sweetness. Slowly they got bigger, turning from green to cream, then pink. The sun, getting hotter each day, encouraged darkening red patches. Dribbling in anticipation, we waited.

As we hoed between the lettuce and cabbage, squashing the caterpillars on the way, we noted that about a dozen strawberries were beginning to look ready for picking. Plump and juicy, they were going to be enjoyed with a drop of double cream poured over them. So we invested 50p in a pot and went to do the picking. And we found that the biggest, reddest and ripest strawberries were gone, leaving empty stalks waving in the breeze. We had got strawberry thieves.

Back home, as we poured the cream over some raspberry jelly, we tried to think of a plan of action. But apart from sitting out on the allotment full time, there wasn't a lot we could do. The fruit, as it ripened, kept on disappearing, and, in spite of spot checks, we never saw the plunderer. That was, until one evening, after watering the runner beans, as we sat in a quiet corner with a flask of tea, we saw a family of blackbirds lined up along a nearby wall. Dad in black plumage, mum and six young in brown. They sat there studying the allotment, not noticing us. With a squawk of command from dad, they flew down, heading straight for the strawberries.

Picking out the best, they began tucking in. Here were our thieves. We jumped up, flapping our arms and they fled to the sanctuary of a nearby tree, where they perched, angrily chattering away at out intervention of their feasting.

By now, at least fifty percent of our precious strawberries had gone to these feathered thieves. Sadie removed the protective netting from off her father's fish pond; the goldfish would have to take their chances at becoming a heron's dinner, and laid it over the plants, anchoring it down at the corners with bits of stick.

But next morning more strawberries had gone. The blackbird family was watching us from their spot on the wall, chattering away, annoyed by our presence. We knew they were responsible for the further losses, but we had no idea how they were doing it.

We hid behind the shed, and waited. The angry chirruping and tail swinging subsided, and then father blackbird flew down, took a look around and called his family. Picking up the odd worm and insect, they all made their way towards the expanse of green netting and gave it a couple of tweaks. Mother and father poked and pulled, the babies watched and waited, so did we. Together, the parents lifted up a small section of netting in their beaks and the babies ducked under, gobbling the fruit. We could not believe it. How on earth had they planned such efficient teamwork? We gave up on the strawberries.

The runner beans, tomatoes, lettuce and cabbage that we'd planted didn't seem to be making the growth that we had hoped. Chewed out holes and torn off strips appeared on the leaves, especially during damp weather. Slugs and snails had discovered the delights of our little allotment. We didn't like to put down pellets and poison the local bird population so Sadie suggested a pot sunk in the ground with a drop of beer inside.

"They can't resist it," she said, "They crawl in have a drink, get drunk and can't crawl out again, and drown."

Sure enough we began to find corpses in the pot, floating in considerably less liquid. But the plants were still being nibbled away in great numbers. The runner beans were losing leaves faster than they could produce them. Stronger action was called for. I suggested a night patrol with a torch and heavy hammer.

"Who's going to do the dirty deed?" asked Sadie. I knew she was a great lover and protector of most living things and was uncomfortable at having to take part in the slugs' splattered demise. Having them die happy in alcohol was just about ok.

"I'll do it, don't you worry, I'll sort them out." I didn't want to see the results of all our hard work in the garden disappearing down their slimy throats.

The next night, holding a small torch in my teeth, and armed with a bucket in one hand and heavy headed hammer in the other, I set up a ruthless campaign of extermination as I prowled after my prey. They were everywhere, dozens of fat, shiny bodies slithering across the grass, stuffing themselves even fatter on our vegetables. Hung from the runner beans was a varied assortment of snails, greedily munching away. This had to be stopped. At the rate they were all feeding their faces, we'd have nothing left.

In front of me was a huge slug, leaving a silvery trail across the grass. I whacked down with the hammer, hoping to flatten it, but so soft was the ground, it just got pushed into the mud. After a few seconds, having recovered from the shock of the assault, it pulled itself together and slid on.

Stronger action was needed. I lined up a couple of chunky bricks, scooped up my prey in a trowel, laid them on the stonework and got whacking. I piled dozens of snails in the bucket, poured them out and bashed away.

But the more I looked, the more I kept finding.

My intense programme of extermination came to a halt around an hour later when a powerful light was suddenly shone in my eyes. Standing there, holding a bucket and a huge hammer, with a torch clenched between my teeth, I must have looked most suspicious to the investigating police officer.

I tried the cheery approach. "Hi, sergeant, I'm just trying to clear this allotment of slugs and snails. They only come out in numbers on damp nights, and they've been eating all our fruit and vegetables. So I'm attempting to get rid of them, permanently, by killing them – with this." I held up the hammer, dripping in slime. He wasn't amused, and shone his torch around the tomatoes and runner beans, presumably looking for human remains.

"A couple of local residents phoned us, concerned that there were some funny goings on here, what with the flashing lights, crashing noises and cries of delight. Instead of all this malarkey, why don't you just put down some slug pellets and leave them to do the work in a quieter fashion?"

"We didn't want the birds to eat the dead slugs and snails and get poisoned. We were simply doing our bit for the environment. It's a quick death and I don't think the RSPCA will be after us."

He grunted. "Well, perhaps you had better finish up for tonight, and try and find a less disturbing way of getting rid of them." So slug and snail disposal became a frequent daytime activity to keep their numbers down.

The ground appeared to be lacking in nourishment, probably due to years of neglect. I said to Sadie, "My father always swore by a good bit of horse manure, especially for his roses. In his day, when he lived in the country, he used to nip out with a bucket and shovel after horses had been ridden by." For us, living in an urban area, such opportunities didn't exist. "Let's go and get some from that donkey sanctuary down the road," suggested Sadie.

After a twenty minute ride, our noses told us we were near. Outside the sanctuary gate stood dozens of sacks, quietly steaming in the morning air. We hastily moved ourselves from downwind to upwind as the pungent odour hit our nostrils.

"I've suddenly got serious doubts about transporting this manure in my car," I said, "I know we use it to carry all sorts of things, but there's a lower limit, below which I will not go, and this is it. Even with the windows open, we couldn't cope with that stink."

Sadie poked at the straw-laden, toffee textured mixture in the assorted re-cycled donkey feed bags and uttered expression of delight at the quality. But I was watching the little pools of fetid brown liquid seeping out from the seams and dribbling onto the pavement.

"I'm not having any of that in my car, it's disgusting." I got back in the driver's seat.

"Its beautiful stuff," said Sadie, "Mix that with a drop of water, get it a bit diluted, let it stand and you've got yourself the finest natural fertiliser in the world, not a chemical in sight. Our plants will love it."

At only 50p a large sack, it did seem to be a bargain. I weakened. We could open all the windows, and if I drove fast enough, the wind coming in the front windows would blow the horrible smell away out the back. I weakened a bit more. If we bought four sacks they would cost £2, much cheaper than buying fertiliser from a shop, and cover a lot more ground. I sniffed. Perhaps it wasn't too bad, after all.

We found a girl mucking out in the stable yard and gave her £2.

"Help yourself," she said, pushing brown slurry around the concrete. I patted the bony nose of an old grey donkey chewing some wisps of hay. He reciprocated the gesture by biting a lump out of my windcheater, the blue plastic swiftly disappearing between a mobile set of thick, yellow teeth.

Going back to the steaming bags, we tried to select the strongest, cleanest sacks. They had all been liberally filled; some had overflowed and were sticky to touch. After selecting four, I wiped my fingers on the long grass and promised myself a good wash when I got home.

We hauled the sacks into the back of the estate car and tried to get them to stand up. Tall and thin, they slumped to one side, spilling bits of brown mess onto those parts of black matting that I had failed to cover with newspapers.

"I don't like this," I muttered to Sadie, "If we don't watch it, they're going to topple over, and I'm not clearing up the mess."

"Oh, go on," she replied, "It's only for about twenty minutes. The road home is fairly straight, just be careful going around corners."

I looked at the bags leaning against the back seats. The plastic creaked as their contents settled lower. I had a nasty feeling about this manure. I grabbed more newspapers from a stack that we used to catch drips from a leaking door when it rained, and pushed the pages about to mop up the drips.

"Be it on your own head," I warned as we got in, hastily opening the windows. I turned the radio on, to try and take our minds off the pong. As we gently moved off down the road, the sacks wobbled but stayed upright. Once onto the dual carriageway, I was able to get up some speed and the smell did seem to be blowing out.

As we sped home, feeling rather pleased with ourselves, we started singing along with some of the popular songs on Southern FM. The sun was shining, it felt good to be alive. The road was mostly on a downhill incline, and the car, apart from a few splutters, was running well, almost touching fifty miles an hour.

Then a cock pheasant decided to take a stroll across the road. Head up, pointed tail up, it strode out onto the tarmac, oblivious to the danger of its imminent death by speeding vehicles. It turned, looked at us heading downhill towards it, and stopped. Without thinking I hit the brakes. My car may have been ancient, with an engine that was a mechanic's nightmare, but it did possess a good set of brakes. We slid to a stop, and, as the bird sauntered regally across to the grass verge, the contents of the manure filled sacks, still in forward motion as velocity triumphed over gravity, cascaded over us.

A long line of cars started to pile up behind us, hooting and flashing their lights, as the interior of mine suddenly acquired a coating of brown, lumpy liquid. The released gases were putrid. I heaved, and forgetting we were still in the middle of the dual carriageway, opened the driver's door and got out, yelling, "I knew it, bloody manure, I knew something would happen. I told you so." I nipped smartly back in again, sitting on the seat with a squelch, as I was almost mown down by dozens of angry motorists who'd had to pull out to avoid me.

I looked at Sadie, sitting there with manure and straw in her hair and brown streaks on her face, resembling a camouflaged commando.

"It's all your fault. My car's ruined; we'll never get it clean."

Something hot and wet was trickling down the back of my neck. In a blazing temper, I wiped the shiny brown coating off the windscreen and pulled into the side of the road. Throwing open all the doors, we surveyed the mess. I glared at Sadie; she looked at me and started laughing.

"You could pass for Worzel Gummidge," she said, trying to free her hair of some of the bits.

I started to giggle, my emotions were bubbling over, I

wanted to cry, but laughter came out instead. We stood by the roadside, smothered from head to foot in what comes out of the rear end of donkeys, and roared with hysterical laughter. Passing motorists must have thought we were mad.

"Well," said Sadie, "At least we've still got some manure left in the sacks, it didn't all come out. There's probably enough to do the job."

We got some long grass from the verge and rubbed ourselves down as best we could, and tried to wipe out the car. The mess was hardening into a beef burger like consistency.

But our trials with the manure were not over. On the way home we had to go over a level crossing. Not any old level crossing, this one is in the Guinness Book of Records as the busiest in the northern hemisphere. The gates were shut almost as long as they were open. And they were shut. A polite notice by the side of the road stated, "Would drivers please switch off their engines whilst waiting, to save fuel and avoid pollution."

We could oblige there, although there was nothing we could do about the pong from the rest of the car. As we sat there, the interior, even with all the windows wide open, got hotter and smellier. The remaining contents of one of the bags gave a few bubbling glugs. I idly scraped my shoe clean on the brake pedal, and began to feel queasy. One long train rumbled through the barriers, but they didn't open. We had to wait for another one going in the opposite direction. It got hotter, the car got smellier.

"I'm going to be sick," I mumbled to Sadie, shifting around in my damp, pungent seat. Another sack gave a glug, and that did it. I threw open the door and threw up. The passengers on the Victoria to Eastbourne train had a grandstand view of a crusty, brown scarecrow doing projectile vomiting over the bonnet of a rusty old car.

As the barriers went up, sick or not, I had to move on,

or the traffic piled up behind would be going nowhere. I heaved, moaned, and still feeling horrible, drove off.

When I got home I threw all my clothes in the washing machine and dived into the shower, letting the water pour all over me until I felt completely clean. The sickening smell still lingered in my nostrils. After putting on fresh, but old clothes, I went to survey the horrors of the car. Sadie, also cleaned up, returned. The vehicle looked a sorry mess; the brown tinted interior now matched the rust tinted exterior. Colour co-ordination.

Throwing the bags into the allotment, we got dozens of buckets of hot water and all the cleaning treatments we could find in the cupboards, then rubbed and scrubbed until our fingers were raw. Then it was all left to dry.

On collecting Jackie from school, she took one look at the brown and grey patched seats, then sniffed and said, "Phew, what died in here?"

"Manure," I replied.

"Oh, go on, pull the other one," she joked.

"Twenty-four carrot manure all over the car."

"Stop being silly mum, what really happened?"

The Car Auction

I had to get a new set of wheels. This old and much treasured car was still getting me from A to B, but bits kept falling off, so there was a rapidly diminishing amount of vehicle returning from B to A. It was fast becoming a moving heap of rust held together by paintwork. My rubbish driving didn't help to keep the bodywork intact, I only had trouble starting, stopping, turning and parking. When I proudly mentioned to Jackie that I'd actually managed to get parked in a small space in the busy town centre in just three moves, she disparagingly said, "What, hit the car in front, hit the car behind, and parked up two feet from the kerb?"

This car was temperamental too. One hint of a frosty morning and it would refuse to start. Whilst Jackie was leaping around, yelling, "Mum, I'm going to be late for school," I would be on my knees in the kitchen rummaging around in the 'Let's bung it in here when we don't know what to do with it' cupboard looking for the Dampstart. It was always lurking at the back, hidden under assorted tins of paint acquired from skips, a bag of old clothes destined for a charity shop and a pair of ragged Wellington boots with a strange odour.

Second-hand car salesmen and I seemed to have widely differing views on vehicle prices, they laughed at my knock down offers, so I decided to take my business to the local auction rooms. I didn't have a clue where to start, so I wandered around dozens of parked cars that were lined up waiting to be sold, trying to appear nonchalant as I peered at dashboards smothered with levers, knobs and widgets that would have made the pilot of a jumbo jet green with envy. I poked under bonnets, pretending to know all about the pitfalls of buying second-hand vehicles. In reality, my knowledge was confined to slurping in some petrol, oil or water when the dials on the dashboard hit the red bits.

Looking around the building, through a maze of exhaust fumes and cigarette smoke, I realised that as a female, I had invaded male territory. There were about three hundred men there, just a handful of women. The men were dressed in cloned clothing of grubby check shirts and oil stained jeans with the odd Arthur Daley sheepskin thrown in.

From his dais the auctioneer pointed out the first vehicle on offer. His mouth then went into overdrive, uttering dozens of words per second, mimicking the incomprehensible jabbering of Australian sheep auctioneers. I tried to keep up with his high-speed verbals, but only managed to comprehend 'lot five in your catalogue' when the bidding took off, and caught up later at 'one thousand pounds.' A brief pause as that car was driven out and when it was replaced by another, he was off again. With more than sixty vehicles to get through in two hours he didn't waste any time.

With a noise like an army tank, a small rust brown car stopped in front of me. A box on wheels obviously put together by students of metalwork with a malicious sense of humour. Undaunted, off went Charlie, the auctioneer. I found I was beginning to keep pace with his verbal velocity.

"What am I bid?" he asked.

No-one was in a rush to buy this sample of Polish technology.

"Come on," he urged, "It's only got 3,000 miles on the clock, MOT for a year, taxed, what more do you want?"

"Fifty quid," yelled a voice from the front, "To take it away for you."

Concurring chuckles rippled around the room. Someone bravely offered £100 and we were away. It was soon up to £110. One of the showroom's team of drivers was attempting to keep the noisy engine running; he probably didn't dare turn it off. Around us, the levels of lead and carbon monoxide had shot up ninety percent. At £170, it all stopped. The new owner crept forward, trying hard to ignore the friendly heckling and Charlie's quip of, "Well, there you are sir, you've just saved yourself a couple of bus fares home."

One of my knowledgeable friends, anxious to help, had said, "Take a magnet with you. If the car has been damaged and repaired with body filler, the magnet won't stick. Run it over the wheel arches and along the sills where rusty patches might have been filled in."

I didn't possess a magnet, one of those had never turned up in a skip, so I asked Sadie if I could borrow the one she used to clean algae from off the sides of her newly acquired goldfish aquarium. I waved it around the rear bumper of an estate I liked the colour of. A powerful attraction immediately developed and, with a thunderous clunk, Sadie's magnet lunged at the metalwork. Heads turned at the sound – I was intently studying a mark on the ceiling.

As bidding progressed I furtively struggled to retrieve the magnet, but it had gained a limpet-like hold onto the metal and refused to budge.

Charlie was still merrily banging his gavel and working his way through the Astras, Escorts, Mondeos and Volvos. I'd have loved any of those but they were all out of my price range. Finally, 'my' estate was next. From the fast declining rows of cars, a harassed driver was struggling to get it started, definitely not a good sign. I became a little wary and greatly reduced my offer price. The death throws of a dying battery produced just enough power to get it going and it chugged up to the dais, Sadie's magnet still firmly attached to the wheel arch.

"Drives well," enthused Charlie. "Got an MOT until October. Only one careful owner."

"And three terrible ones," muttered a voice behind me.

After an opening bid of £300, I was tempted to make an offer, but thick, sooty black smoke was belching out of the exhaust. This made me keep my hands in my pockets, so did everyone else. The gavel banged down at £400 and my chances were gone along with the magnet.

Tony's Death

Jackie strolled in with her best friend Emma, they both had big smiles.

"Guess where we've been today?"

I instantly knew the answer.

"You've been to see your father, haven't you?"

She nodded.

"He was really pleased to see me, and said to Barbara, his wife, 'Look this is my daughter, Jackie.' He's even given me this watch."

In her clenched hand she was holding an elderly timepiece that had seen better days, but I could see that, to her, it was a priceless gift.

For a number of years we had known where Tony was living, a search through the telephone directory had revealed the address, which was only a mile away. I had always said that if she wanted to make contact with her dad, I had no problem with that.

"We cycled to daddy's house then lost our nerve and rode away. But we went back and tried to pluck up courage to ring the bell. Emma knocked and ran away, leaving me to do the explaining. He was so excited at seeing me and wants me to go to dinner next weekend. And he's married."

She visited on a regular basis, and when she mentioned that she was soon going on holiday, he slipped her a £10 note. She was invited to their Christmas dinner, but they both found it increasingly hard, after a fourteen year gap, to become used to a father/daughter relationship. But she regularly got on her bike and rode down the cycle track "To see my daddy."

Whilst on holiday she sent him a postcard asking him to get in touch when she returned. When he didn't, she decided to stop visiting. When he forgot her birthday in

May, it seemed that the relationship had run its course. Bitterly disappointed, she shrugged her shoulders and remarked, "Well he never really was good father material."

With Christmas a short time away, she wrote him a long, chatty letter, enclosed a photograph and waited for a reply. It never came.

I received a phone call from Barbara's daughter–in – law, "I'm so sorry to have to tell you this but Tony died last night, he had a stroke." I suddenly felt very cold. Seconds later Jackie walked in the door. Holding on to the moment, I said, "Darling, I've got some very sad news for you, your daddy died last night." She burst into tears, and sobbed, "I wish I'd told him I loved him, now he'll never know," then ran into the garden where Emma was waiting. As a small child Emma had also lost her dad, so she could understand Jackie's distress. They hugged and talked.

After a while Jackie decided to telephone Barbara, and after a short conversation she handed me the phone saying, "We've both been invited to daddy's funeral and the 'do' afterwards. I very much want to go, do you?"

I found that my hands were shaking as I took hold of the phone. I struggled to find the right words.

"Oh, Barbara, I'm sorry. Are you all right?" She seemed very collected and discussed the funeral arrangements in a matter of fact way, adding, "Would you like to come?"

"Jackie would very much like to be there, but it wouldn't be right for me to turn up."

That night I had trouble sleeping. In a state of being half awake and half asleep, I felt my bed sink a little on one side, as if someone was sitting there. A voice whispered, "You look after her for me," and slowly the weight lifted. In my dream-like state, I groped for the switch on the bedside lamp, somehow expecting to see Tony standing there. I could smell the old familiar scent of his body. But the room was empty. "I will, I will," my heart answered.

Jackie chose flowers to be sent for the funeral, and on the day I drove her down to the Crematorium. A group were gathered at the entrance, waiting for the arrival of the hearse. She joined them and gave Barbara a hug. I stood by my parked car, a distance away from the mourners. I couldn't just drive off, as I'd intended. I waited. A shiny black vehicle nudged its way through the entrance and slowly drove down the narrow gravel track. In the back was a coffin. Tears welled up in my eyes as I realised that inside was the cold body of a man I'd once loved so much.

The vehicle stopped by the main doors, and four sombre suited men dismounted and carefully slid the coffin out, hitching it up onto their shoulders. They slowly walked into the building, followed first by Barbara and Jackie, then the rest of the mourners. The big doors shut.

I stood there. Something then compelled me to get into my car and drive. I returned to the area of our little roses round the door cottage, and walked down a rough path that we had often wheeled baby Jackie along, and came to a cosy sheltered spot we'd used for picnics. With tartan rug laid out, we'd both sat and proudly watched our little girl pick daisies and dandelions, offer her daddy a bite of her sandwich, and point up to the clouds scurrying across the sky.

Nothing had changed there. I sat on the grass and listened to the trees softly sighing in the breeze. My bottom lip trembled and I sobbed from the bottom of my heart. For years I carried a hate for Tony for the grief he had caused, but now, at his death, the circle had been closed. There was just sadness left.

Picking Jackie up from the house where friends and family had collected for drinks and nibbles, I nervously hesitated before ringing the bell. Barbara opened the door. She looked at me and burst into tears. The two of us clung together, weeping for a man, who, in spite of his imperfections, we had both dearly loved and lost.

Jackie had perhaps suffered the greater loss and as she looked at the two of us, she simply said, "If only…."

Looking For A Man In My Life

I started to feel my age. I might have been the mother of a teenage daughter who strangers presumed was my granddaughter, and I had come to accept that I could live without sex, but couldn't do without my glasses. My joints were more accurate meteorologists than the national weather service and I'd quit holding my stomach in, no matter who walked into the room.

But a man hadn't featured in my life for some while, and living in a seaside town renowned for its octogenarian generation, the only ones I came across, whilst serving behind shop counters, were either pushing Zimmer frames, hobbling along with walking sticks, or they'd forgotten what they'd come in to buy.

'Marriage,' said comedian Billy Connolly, 'is a wonderful invention, but then, so is a bicycle repair kit.' Groucho Marx observed, 'The husband who wants a happy marriage should learn to keep his mouth shut and his cheque book open.'

I half-heartedly perused the "Let's Find Love" columns of the local Free-Ad. 'Men Looking for Women' was overflowing with presumably desperate males. Must be someone in there for me, it would be a definite plus if they had a pulse, their own teeth and an offshore bank account. I began to read the pages, and was soon 'cracking their codes.'

'Shy guy, 54, 6ft 1in, seeks girl who wants to get to know him....' – Unable to sustain any decent conversation.

'Don't think twice...' – The others have run in the opposite direction.

'Older guy, separated...' - Looking for a good time, even if the divorce hasn't come through yet.

'Looking for a biker lady...' - Likes doing it up against the Harley Davison.

'Genuine single dad...' - a dozen offspring by five different women scattered around the area.

'Outgoing, adventurous male, fancies a drink, seeks similar female...' – So we can go out and get ratted together.

'Young looking 42 year old, let me make you dinner...' – dreadful cooking drove prospective partners away.

'Sentimental, romantic, short hair, piercings...' - Bald headed yob with ironmongery shoved into a multitude of weird places.

'Let's see where it goes?' - Straight to the bedroom.

'Likes pubs and restaurants' – drinks and eats a lot.

'Easy going male, many interests in life' – bone idle, enjoys threesomes.

Young 70, enjoys flying, drinks out, socialising' – Wants someone to push his wheelchair for him.

'Affectionate and tactile guy' – Hands all over you.

'Passionate and experienced guy, looking for down to earth, mature lady' – How quickly can he get his leg over?

'New experiences with an adventurous mate' – How quickly can he get both legs over, accompanied by a bag full of sex toys.

'Someone to chat to' – Boring.

'Well built' – Fat.

'I'm 37' - At least 45.

'Cuddly' – large beer gut.

'Gentleman' – hasn't had sex since 1999.

'Idealistic' - crashing bore.

'Likes nights in by the fire' – cheapskate.

'Non-judgmental' – Internet porn addict.

'Passionate' – on Viagra.

'Successful' – has his own set of power tools.

'Wealthy' – drug dealer.

'Honest' – rude.

'Outdoor type' – doesn't wash.

'Romantic' – takes socks off for sex.

'Dave, 58, easygoing, friendly, in good shape, enjoys quiet nights in, loves photography' – How soon can he get your clothes off for some naughty nude pictures?

'Share you life with me, a passionate gardener' - Married to his allotment.

'A boy at heart, loves mountain biking, skiing, riding, active weekends' – Member of the Mile High Club.

I began to realise that the word 'partner' meant any shack-up sexual relationship that lasted longer than three days.

Then Charles came on the scene. A few years older than me, but he'd scrubbed up well. In spite of his mature years, his features still sported a rugged handsomeness. He bred budgerigars and was in and out buying bags of bird seed from the pet food section of the DIY shop. He started telling me about all the prizes his budgies had won at shows and at each visit, his stays became longer. Was he, in some awkward way, trying to get round to chatting me up? I quite liked him, but was he partner material? I didn't know. At my age I had to accept that men were like parking spaces - the good ones were already taken.

Then he asked me out. I said, 'ok' thinking it was just for a drink and see where it goes from there, but he added, "It's a surprise."

I wanted to know where I was going, so I could dress accordingly. Maybe to a nice restaurant and a walk along the seafront afterwards, or a drive to a country pub? He didn't look the type who'd plump for a pint, a packet of crisps and a game of darts. So I chose a dress that might have passed for smart ten years previously, with a stylish designer label cream coat I'd discovered in a charity shop.

The doorbell rang; he stood there wearing a suit that might have passed as smart ten years previously. He smiled and said, "Are you ready?" As I got close I could smell Brut, he'd obviously liberally splashed it on.

"Yes, I'm dying to see this surprise."

I looked up and down the street for his car. Parked outside was an old green Morris van. 'I hope it's not that one,' I thought to myself. But it was. He went and politely opened the passenger door. The two seats looked as if they hadn't been touched by a clean cloth for years; a cream coat was a bad choice. Black would have been better. As I got in I noticed a little lamp in the well on the passenger's side.

"What's that for?" I asked, trying to get comfortable in my hard, unyielding seat.

"Oh, the van's heating packed up long ago, I just light it for some warmth when I'm travelling in cold weather. I take my budgies in this to shows all around the country. It's ideal for transporting their show cages in special carrying cases."

At the back, I noticed a pile of old blankets, I hoped they were used for keeping his precious birds warm and hadn't been packed in the hope we'd have a get together later on.

We went out of town by the pretty route, along the seafront and over the Downs. It was to be a country pub, then. Half an hour later, we were passing through Brighton. This was before the A27 became a by-pass. Then it was a tiny road snaking up through a built-up residential area, with just enough room, at one point, for two cars to pass each other.

The van started to judder, and clouds of steam puffed out from under the bonnet. The vehicle ground to a halt halfway up this narrow, winding hill.

"I think we've run out of water," explained Charles, apologetically. I could only think, 'Oh no, not again. What is it about my dates, cars and loss of water?' Angry hooting from behind made him realise that we were holding up half the motorists in southern England who were endeavouring to keep on moving westwards. The long stream of traffic coming down the hill certainly wasn't going to give way. Charles got out and made appropriate 'sorry' gestures to the car behind. The driver made appropriate rude gestures in return. As the hissing steam formed a cloud over the bonnet, the pair of us stood there and tried to think of a game plan.

"There's an antiques shop at the bottom of this hill," said Charlie, "Maybe we could borrow a container and some water from them." He took off, leaving me to run the brunt of the shouting, hooting and varying two fingered signals. I distanced myself from the scene and sat on a garden wall about fifty yards away, nonchalantly swinging my legs and kicking the brickwork. A short time later, Charlie returned, holding a large glass vase full of water.

"They made me buy this, cost me a pound," he said angrily, pouring the liquid into the radiator. "The cheek of some people. They said, no sale, no water."

After some encouragement, the van started and we progressed up the hill, still heading westwards. Obviously we were not going to be eating out, or going to a show, in Brighton. Must be Hove, then. It was. The dog track. Hundreds of people standing around on cold, wet concrete, whooping and yelling as lithe greyhounds hurtled around a course chasing after a stuffed, moving rabbit. Charles was in his element, I was bored silly. "Isn't this great?" he asked, his face registering pure pleasure.

"Not really my scene," was all I could think of in answer, but he didn't notice my lack of enthusiasm. It started to rain. My cream coat had been made for its looks; its water repellent properties were rubbish. I just wanted to go home.

"Shall we get something to eat," he enquired between races, and I perked up at the thought of some decent food, nice wine and clean, white tablecloths. But he headed towards the burger van. Fish and chips in plastic boxes with wooden spoons just didn't cut it with me, especially when he asked if I wanted any ketchup, and spattered my coat with red blobs when he passed over the bottle.

"Wasn't that great," he enthused and patted my knee as we set off home. I grunted, and removed his hand that was now sliding up my thigh. I hoped the lack of water situation did not re-occur on the return journey. It was now dark and we hadn't topped up the jug. Mind you, we could have filled it up from the rain that was now pelting down, turning the road into a river.

Before you could say, "Have you got a condom?" he'd turned sharp left off the A27 and dived down a rough country lane. He stopped the van and plonked his hand on my knee again.

"What about it?" he enquired.

"What about what?" I snapped back.

"Don't you fancy a bit of the other?" he muttered, trying to kiss me with sloppy wet lips.

I pushed him away.

"No, I don't. Get off me and let's get home."

I wasn't going to be bought with a night at the dogs, a bag of chips and an uncomfortable ride in a shaky old van.

"Go on, I'm not playing your games, let's get home."

"You're nothing but a tease."

"No, I'm not. You invited me on a surprise outing. Just because I said I'd come, it doesn't mean I'm going to climb into the back of this dirty old van and have sex with you. I'm not that kind of person."

"You're a teasing old cow," he retorted as he started the engine.

"I don't care what you think, take me home."

Easier said than done, as he revved the engine, the wheels spun and dug themselves into the muddy ground.

We were well and truly stuck. It was close to midnight, and there was definitely no traffic in this tiny lane. Charles started to panic, "I've got to get home soon." I didn't have that problem with Jackie; she was on a sleepover with her best friend.

"Why have you got to get home?" I had to ask, "Is there someone waiting for you?"

"No, no, I've just got to get home, that's all."

He wouldn't be drawn on the reason.

"Look, can you get out and give the van a bit of a push from the back, if I run the engine we might be able to get ourselves out of here."

"You must be joking. It's pouring with rain, we're stuck in inches of mud. We haven't a hope of getting free unless someone gives us a pull out."

But there was a note of desperation in his voice, so against my better judgement, I opened the door and climbed out. I sank into the quagmire and got soaked as I squelched around to the rear of the vehicle. Having put my shoulder to the metal work I shouted, "O.K. give it a go."

Stupid decision. He revved the engine far too much, the spinning back wheels dug themselves even further into the sludge, which then sprayed all over my cream coat, turning it shit coloured.

"You stupid......." I was so furious, I couldn't find the right words. As I stepped forward, there was a squelch as one of my shoes parted company with my drenched foot and stuck fast in the mud. I groped around to retrieve it whilst Charles kept on saying, "I'm sorry, I'm sorry."

"So you should be. Look at my coat, my best shoes are ruined, and here we are stuck in the middle of nowhere. What are you going to do about it?"

"We've got no choice, we're going to have to walk back to the main road and see if we can thumb a lift."

"Who's going to give us a lift, I'm that filthy, no-one

would want me messing up their car seats."

"I must get home." He climbed out and started walking along the track.

The rain eased as we stumbled along. When we reached the dual carriageway and tried to get a lift from the few passing vehicles, no one wanted to stop. Not surprising, as we must have both looked awful. Fortunately, a white van man took pity on us and was even good enough to drop me at my front door. I was so furious at the whole sorry episode that I was in no mood to say 'goodbye' to Charles.

I didn't see him for weeks, until one of his budgie keeping friends came into the shop. Curiously enquiring as to his whereabouts, the friend said, "Oh, he won't be buying any more seed. Some weeks ago he got home in the early hours of the morning in a dishevelled state; his wife found out the van was parked up a country lane, discovered a large tin of Brut in the glove compartment, accused him of having an affair and let all his prize budgies out."

Angel And The Wedding

"How nice, we've got an invitation to a friend's wedding." I showed Jackie the smart invitation card.

"Shall we go?"

"Oh, yes, mum, that would be lovely; I've never been to a wedding."

As the service was to be held at one of the grandest hotels on the seafront, we felt that we should really dress up for the occasion. Being used to wearing everyday clothes, donning posh outfits seemed strange at first, but we both reckoned that we didn't look too bad.

I felt that we couldn't use the old car for transport on this occasion, in fact the front door porter would probably have asked us to remove it from their car park, as, huddled between the waxed and polished Rovers, Bentleys and Audis, our battered, rust riddled vehicle would definitely have lowered the tone of this hotel. So we enjoyed the luxury of a taxi and strolled together into the foyer, looking for a sign that would give directions to the room where the wedding was to be held. A crowd was heading for a sign that said 'BAR' in big flashing lights. We followed. Smartly suited staff were dispensing drinks, and our order for a lemonade and small sherry were quickly processed.

"Is madam paying by card or cash," enquired the young man serving us. I didn't wish to tell him I didn't 'do cards' and, having glimpsed the astoundingly large bill for two drinks, felt tempted to say, 'Neither,' as I began to wonder if there was enough money in my purse to cover the cost. Whilst other customers at this 4 star establishment were pulling out fifty pound notes or gold coloured cards to pay for their orders, I was discreetly trying to count out my coins to pay for mine.

"The bride is on her way, she will be here in a minute,"

someone shouted, and we all rushed to the big windows to watch her arrival. And we weren't disappointed. Along the seafront came a fairy-tale glass coach pulled by two plumed, and lively grey horses. As they were brought to a halt outside the front entrance, a limousine nudged in behind the coach containing the Matron of Honour, Chief Bridesmaid and four tiny bridesmaids.

Whilst the stable groom held the horses' heads, the traditionally dressed coachman opened the carriage door and helped the bride and her father to dismount. Her wedding dress, a froth of cream silk, had a long train, which the little ones were encouraged to hold onto.

And so, to the sounds of the Wedding March being belted out by an enthusiastic organist, the graceful entourage entered the building, heading towards the wedding–themed, flower-filled ballroom. Our friend, the nervous husband – to - be, was out in the garden, smoking on what was probably his tenth cigarette during the last thirty minutes. To shouts of "Come on, quick, she's here," from his Best Man, he dumped the dog- end in amongst the dahlias and scurried to his position in front of the vicar.

He waited for his future wife, her father, Matron of Honour, Chief Bridesmaid and the quartet of little bridesmaids to enter the room. But - they failed to appear. As the music played on, and on, most of the invited audience were unaware of the cause of the hold – up in the corridor.

One of the bridesmaids, four year old Angel, with her fair curly hair and big blue eyes, looked perfect for this part. But looks can be deceiving. Angel could have moments of being kindergarten's answer to Terminator 2, and right then she obviously decided that being a bridesmaid was definitely not in her job description.

The procession was forced to halt as she threw down her portion of the train, crossed her arms, pouted her lips and shouted, "Shan't." Then she sat down on the floor.

The Chief Bridesmaid, her carer for the occasion, had wisely been ready for the possibility of rebellious tantrums, and got her walking again by bribing her with a piece of chocolate that just happened to be in her cream purse.

But although Angel was now upright, she wouldn't go back to her rightful place in the procession. The bride's bouncing skirt held more attractions; Angel grabbed the hem, lifted it up, and peering underneath, loudly announced to the amused congregation, "Look, my mummy's got blue knickers."

With what appeared to be muttered threats from the Chief Bridesmaid, Angel quietly picked up her corner of the train and the procession carried on, heading towards the smiling vicar and waiting husband-to-be. But, a few seconds into the service, even before the words, "We are gathered here today......" were uttered, Angel wrenched off her flower embellished headband and threw it at the vicar. In spite of a quick tackle by the Chief Bridesmaid, her posy followed the same route. By the time the service had finished and the wedded couple were heading towards the Reception Room, Angel had systematically ripped most of the frills off her dress, to the horror of Peggy, the dressmaker, who had spent weeks laboriously making all the cream silk dresses for this wedding. Armed with a few handy safety pins, she somehow managed to sort out Angel's diminishing frock, in readiness for some more Wedding Pictures.

In a rare moment of sunshine, the bride and groom posed on the front steps of the hotel, then by the carriage, with their respective families, and, of course with the bridesmaids. But there was now one bridesmaid short. Whilst the photographer had fussed and puffed to get the people and pictures right, a bored Angel had slipped away from the care of the Chief Bridesmaid and gone missing. But before anyone could start searching for her, one of the bar staff came rushing up, saying, "I wonder if anyone can come and help? One of your little bridesmaids has got her head stuck in the bar balcony railings."

Unfazed by her captive predicament, Angel had discovered a new game, seeing how many puffs it took to demolish the numerous spiders' webs hung around her on the ironwork. After we'd carefully squirted a few drops of washing up liquid, courtesy of the hotel kitchen, around Angel's head, we then went through the delicate operation of trying to get her unscrewed. Her ears did get in the way, greatly hindering a backward pull, but with the help of another application of washing up liquid, she finally slid out.

Chief Bridesmaid managed to get hold of a towel and tried to clean Angel up. But her appearance was now past the point of no return, it looked as if she had been dressed in front of an aircraft propeller. After a few angry words from her worried mother, who had seized the opportunity to have a quick smoke on the balcony, Angel rubbed her bruised and oily head and reluctantly said, "Sorry, mummy."

She then spotted the liberal display of food.

"Mummy, please can I have a sausage roll?"

"Go on then, but you stay where we can see you."

Chief Bridesmaid was again roped in to shadow Angel, but decided that one little girl sitting quietly on a stool, with a sausage roll in each hand, wasn't going to go far. She turned and carried on flirting with one of the good looking, young male guests.

We watched as Angel apparently decided to sample as many of the foods as she could. A trail of half eaten sausage rolls, chewed chicken legs and tooth marked sandwiches were soon scattered along the white tablecloth. Then she sampled the contents of one of the numerous half filled glasses that were around, and, with a crafty look to see if her 'carer' was still being chatted up, decided to carry on with the drinking.

The alcohol soon took effect; we saw her slide off the chair and disappear under the table. Jackie lifted up one of the drapes to check things out and found Angel was taking great delight in stroking the legs of some of the seated guests. Unaware that she was there, a few misinterpreted this action, and, after some meaningful glances, paired off, staggered drunkenly into the garden, disappearing behind a gushing water feature of naked cherubs.

Although apparently having got bored with twanging a few suspenders and trying to tie shoelaces together, Angel refused to come out from under the table. Her 'carer' accompanied by her admirer, sat down and pulled up the edge of the tablecloth to see what was going on. As nothing appeared amiss, they started indulging in a lengthy, and passionate, kissing session.

But by now Angel had run out of steam; too tired to seize the opportunity to play up any more, she fell asleep. A while later, the Chief Bridesmaid, having suddenly remembered her responsibilities, hastily hitched up the top of her strapless dress to a respectable level, and peeped under the table again.

There lay Angel, curled up on the carpet, a smile on her face and sick down the front of her dress.

"Ah," said her mother, gazing fondly at her youngest offspring, "Isn't she just a little angel."

The Store

"Do you want to earn a bit of extra money over Christmas?" asked Jackie. Growing up fast, she had secured a part - time job shelf stacking in a national cut price store.

"They're looking for temporary staff to work in the evenings, tidying up, filling the shelves, cleaning up the shop floor. I know that you've got your two part-time day jobs, but this company is paying good money, although it's only for about six weeks. There might even be more work available after Christmas."

Already working from 8.30am to 4.30pm, and earning enough to get by, I could have said 'no,' but I opened my mouth and the words, "I'd love to, I'm only sitting watching the TV in the evenings," came out. I surprised myself for making such a rash decision, but later on I would be so glad that I did.

The hours were from 6 pm until whenever, sometimes as late as 3 am, coping with the effects of busy times of the year. The building was a huge warehouse selling a variety of goods ranging from clothes, books, household items, toys and sweets. After a day of busy sales the goods on the shop floor would be in an absolute mess. It took an age to tidy and re-stock all the shelves, then clean the floor and wipe down any grubby work surfaces.

We started to find a number of empty hangers thrown under the clothing rails, a sure sign we had shoplifters who had discovered a weak spot in the shop's minimal security system. Realising were no CCTV cameras, they'd come in through a two way door along from the check-out exit, hide between the clothes rails, carefully remove baby outfits or underwear from off the hangers, stuff them in their pockets or bags, then walk out, unchallenged.

Beth, who was in charge of this section, had never, in thirty years of retailing, had to cope with such blatant thieving, but said, "Well, I'm not surprised, given the lack of security." On the run up to Christmas, everyone was so desperately busy; there was no time to keep a permanent watch on this section. Just closing up the two way door might have cut down on the problems, but it seemed head office didn't want to shut out any customers, so it stayed open, and the loss of goods continued.

We occasionally caught the odd thief, took the goods off them and banned them, but they just got their mates to come in instead. None of this ever came to court. Then Dick, the manager, made another discovery. Outside the rear delivery entrance stood an unlocked waste disposal bin As he delved into the bin's contents, hunting for an item he believed had been mistakenly thrown out, he found, right at the bottom, a plastic bag containing quantities of the company's children's clothes. One of the newly engaged, temporary staff was stealing the outfits, putting them in black bags, and placing them in the refuse bin. After work, they would nip around to the back, lift out the stolen goodies and sell them on a market stall. The employee was sacked, having confessed that she had only gone for the job to see how much she could steal. Dick put a lock on the bin, although the words 'horse' and 'stable door' did come to mind.

But the thieving on the shop floor went on; it seemed that as much was being smuggled out the front door as was being delivered through the back. One evening, coming into work, I noticed a wide advertising strip had been placed on a balcony that ran across part of the rear of the shop. It featured some advertising blurb about the business and showed two happy smiling faces with rather peculiar eyes, which appeared to be moving. On closer inspection I found two of the night crew were concealed behind the poster, watching out for prospective thieves by peering down onto the shop floor through the cut out holes. They did catch a few people and barred them, which didn't help much, as so many had now been banned, the checkout staff sunk below a sea of 'don't let them in here' faces. The pile of empty, discarded, hangers grew daily and the problem was never effectively resolved.

By Christmas the shop was fantastically busy, staff were offered 20% discount on goods bought in-house, so Jackie and I, revelling in our good financial fortune, recklessly spent £100 each on gifts and decorations. We had never felt so rich. And we were delighted when we were both offered a continuation of employment afterwards.

A few months later I would be so glad I had taken this extra job.

The Holiday

A holiday, that's what we needed, a holiday. "How about a few days away at a holiday park?" suggested Jackie. "My best friend Lisa said her mum Linda was talking about taking a short break, maybe we could all go together?"

So, now we could afford this little luxury, we booked up, packed our cars with cases and headed west, to a holiday park deep in the Hampshire countryside. Jackie and I, Linda, Lisa and her brother Chris.

By Saturday evening, a short time after checking in, we felt as if we'd been there for weeks. The weather had been unusually hot, more like July than April. Linda and I sat on the veranda that enclosed our enormous mobile home, and enjoyed the rural tranquillity as the purple dusk enfolded us.

The quiet of the evening was broken only by the splash of the shower and the whirr of hair dryers as the girls embarked on the marathon task of getting ready for a lively session of partying and entertainment at the clubhouse.

And then it happened. All the lights in the park went out. There were anguished screams of "My hair dryer's not working," from the bedroom and "The shower's stopped," from the bathroom.

We waited in the velvet darkness for someone in authority to pull a switch or put a plug back in and return our lights. It didn't happen. So we lit the gas fire and the flickering flame gave us just enough illumination to see our way around the lounge. On a shelf we spotted a tiny brass lamp with a diminutive candle in it. Made more for show than use, the delicate case defied our fumbling attempts to open it and light the candle.

We pulled at the top, and prised at the base, before

144

discovering a miniscule hinge on one of the glass doors. Once inside, we found that the tall, thin, tapering candle went right up into the dome of the lamp, so it had to be taken out to be lit. Easier said than done. The damp wick was reluctant to stay alight and when we did get it 'in situ' it kept going out. Ten spent matches later someone hit upon the bright idea of cutting a bit off the bottom of the candle so it would have more space to burn efficiently. And it worked, although it was emitting so little light we began to wonder why we'd bothered. Then, as we shut the glass door, a cloud of acrid, black smoke wisped out of the hole in the top and set off the smoke alarm above.

We leapt around, waving towels and cloths in the air, in an effort to stop the noise. Jackie grabbed the lamp by its handle, then screamed, "Oh, this is red hot," and threw it out of the open door. It disintegrated across the lawn. But the alarm stopped.

An hour later, we made enquiries at the park office about the situation, and were told, "We're sorry we have a major electrical fault, but hopefully it won't take too long to put right. We went back, and by the luminous dial of Lisa's watch, crawled around the garden gathering up the fragmented lamp. Put back together, we found that it burned reasonably well if we left the little door open and the dome off.

We all sat and stared at the flames. Someone said, "I spy with my little eye...."But as no-one could really see much, this game didn't last long. There was now only about half the candle left.

"I don't think we are going to have light for much longer," I said, and, desperate for something to do, we started a sweepstake on the candle's lifespan. Ten pence each, winner takes fifty pence.

We made up our minds to go down to the still lit clubhouse. We would have to try and get ready as best we could in the darkness. The girls, bereft of working hair dryers, knelt down in front of the fire, desperately trying to brush their wet tresses into some kind of manageable shape. A strong smell of singeing hair hit our nostrils.

But we then hit another snag. Not only did we have no light, we had no water either. The electrically driven water pumps were also out of action. But we weren't going to be defeated now. A quick rub down with flannels dampened with bottled water, followed by a change of clothes and bountiful squirts of body spray started to get us in party mood.

Making up our faces was more of a challenge as we each attempted to apply makeup in a mirror, assisted by someone else holding the lamp close by, a lamp whose flame was now down to its final, wobbly, glimmer.

It keeled over thirty-seven minutes after we had started the sweepstake. Linda pocketed her 50p winnings and we stumbled out of the door, using the luminous dial on Lisa's watch to find the keyhole.

The darkness was absolute as we groped our way down the winding road to the brilliantly lit clubhouse. When we were ten yards from the entrance all the lights suddenly came on. Loud cheers could be heard from all around the park. Rushing back to our mobile home to make ourselves more presentable, we were horrified to discover that, with our damp frizzy hair, blindly selected clothes and dodgy make up, we looked totally bizarre.

We had a gloriously enjoyable week's holiday, but as we drove home, I wasn't to know what an awful letter I was going to find amongst the mail scattered on the doormat.

The Repossession?

The letter, from Wynne Baxter, Business Recovery Group, didn't mince its words.

RE YOUR AFFAIRS IN BANKRUPTCY.

At the time of your bankruptcy it was accepted that there was no equity in your property. However, since 1992, property prices have increased and I now believe that there is considerable equity in the property and this asset should be realised and the distribution made to your creditors.

I have asked the Alliance and Leicester to provide me with a mortgage redemption statement and I will request that you provide me with a current valuation of the property. A local estate agent will normally do this free of charge.

On the information I have on file, I estimate that the sum required to pay your creditors, including statutory interest of 8% since November 1992 and the fees and disbursements, to be in the region of £30,000. I must stress that this is only an estimate as not all creditors have proved their debt. If the equity in the property is less than the estimated figure, I am required to realise the amount of the equity only.

Richard M. Samuels – Trustee.

"I don't believe this," I said, showing the letter to Jackie, "Its ten years since I went bankrupt, and now, after all this time, the trustees want me to sell my house so creditors from my bankruptcy can be paid. This is like some kind of sick joke. Surely it can't be correct to chase after me for so much money after this length of time. The original debt was only £10,000."

"What are we going to do, mum?" A tear trickled down her cheek and I could see her bottom lip was trembling. "Are we going to be homeless and have to live on the streets in cardboard boxes?"

I couldn't tell her that at sixty-two there appeared little chance of me being able to re-mortgage and I certainly didn't have £30,000 in the bank. It seemed a hopeless situation. The house was the only thing that I had in the world to pass onto Jackie as her inheritance. I'd fought so hard to keep it and now it looked as if it was going to be snatched away.

Opening an old suitcase where I'd kept all the original bankruptcy paperwork, I searched for any evidence that the demand for £30,000 was unenforceable. My heart sank when I came across a booklet I'd been given, "A guide to Bankruptcy," which clearly stated:-

"When you are discharged there may still be assets that you owned either when your bankruptcy began or which you acquired before your discharge, which the trustee has not yet dealt with. These may include your home.....

These assets are still controlled by the trustee, who can deal with them AT ANY TIME IN THE FUTURE. This may not be for a number of years AFTER YOUR DISCHARGE. ......These assets could be claimed to pay your creditors."

That was it; I was well and truly screwed. All the years of work and worry were for nothing. Jackie was inconsolable about losing the only home she had known for most of her life, and that was made worse when my enquiry about council housing was met with the dismal information that there was a 3-5 year waiting list for accommodation.

My hopes were dashed even further, when an estate agent valued my house and said it was worth around £85,000. As the balance of the mortgage owed was £35,200, this meant there was plenty of equity in the property.

Renting was a possible option, but I'd always felt that this was throwing good money away for nothing. There had to be a way out of this problem. Looking at the claims, which amounted to £30,180.74, I noticed that a number of the trading firms listed on the original bankruptcy documents had long gone out of business. The original debt to them was about £1,500, at least, I innocently thought, enough to bring the bill down a lesser amount.

"What happens here," I asked the trustees, "When these companies no longer exist?"

"The government takes the money instead."

"There's an amount of nearly £4,000 labelled Ad Valorum (15%), what is that?"

"This is a fee charged by the Secretary of State and is a statuary requirement."

"So that means the government takes this money, too?"

"Yes, and there's nearly £10,000 in statuary interest @8% that's been added on over the 10 years."

"Don't tell me - the government takes that too?"

"Yes."

There was no getting out of this whopping bill; in fact it was growing by the month.

Sick to the pit of my stomach I tried to think of a way out. Wanting to make the situation go away, even for a few hours, I said to Jackie, "I'm off to bed to sleep on the problem. Maybe things will look better in the morning."

But stress had played havoc with my body. Normally I could watch TV in the lounge until 3am, and get away with four hours sleep before getting up for work at 7.30am. But, as it was before midnight, I plumped for a hot chocolate and a warm lavender scented bubble bath.

I couldn't give up the TV completely, so I switched on the portable, hoping that an hour's viewing of boring re-runs of fifty year old films would soften the problems and guarantee a good night's sleep. I settled down, mesmerised by the flickering screen and tried to ignore the dark pain in my stomach. My eyelids soon began to droop. Dopily, I groped for the remote, zapped off the television and snuggled down.

Three seconds later and I was wide awake. I tossed and turned, trying to get comfortable. I settled for the foetal position, with my relaxed hands tucked into my legs, and quickly came to the conclusion that my lower limbs were in dire need of an intense course of hair removal. I turned over.

I can't snooze laid on my back, because in that position, at best, I snore loud enough to register on the Richter Scale, at worst, sleep apnoea clutches and closes my throat, causing near suffocation. But I decided to give it a go for a while.

Laid out like a corpse, I tried a deep breathing session, recommended for relaxed sleep. Breathe in, hold for a count of six, breathe out, and hold for another count of six. After only a few sessions of sniffing in all the oxygen around my bed, I became breathless and dizzy.

Then a twinge started in the big toe of my left foot. After a few painful spasms, it jerked up at right angles to my body. I tried pushing it down with the heel of my right foot, but the big toe was not going to give up without an under-blanket standoff. The cramp spread to its neighbours, and I then had the agony of all five toes pointing skywards. The threat of even more tightening muscles started to spread up my left leg. I tried pointing my left foot, attempting to force the toes back into their natural position, but the pain was so bad, I had to give up. Just as I was about to leap out of bed and have a go at walking back to normality, the muscles all suddenly stopped pulling, and relaxed. I breathed a sigh of relief and turned over onto my left side.

I could hear my heart beating. A regular thump, thump, thump, forcing my life blood around my body. Thump, thump. I started to listen carefully to the beats, convinced that there was a thump occasionally being missed out. Mild panic set in, was I heading for a heart attack? The thumps were now going at a greater speed as adrenaline leeched into my system, called upon to cope with my increased bout of anxiety. I broke out into a bit of a sweat. I was convinced my heart was not working properly, there were some definite gaps between the beats, followed by three fast thumps all coming together. Should I grab the phone and call an ambulance? But I tried to lie quietly and wait: soon the rhythm dropped back to normal. I turned over.

The clubs and pubs started to turn out. Noisy revellers began cavorting down the street. Normally, I wouldn't have heard them, being engrossed in some noisy war film on the downstairs TV. But, in the quiet of the bedroom, I could hear every vomit, swear word, giggle and scream. As they passed below my open bedroom window, I hoped they wouldn't ravage my little blue Fiesta parked outside. After a previous drunken session, I found one of my wing mirrors had been torn off and stuffed in the open aperture of a nearby post box. That night, as I looked out of the window, their entertainment was to be 'kick a garden gnome down the road.' But, they soon lost interest when his head disintegrated, the red hat going down a drain and his beard over a garden wall. I wasn't sure what they did with his fishing rod.

I climbed back into bed, pulled up the bedding, took a deep breath and tried to settle again. Then my stomach started a symphony of gurgles, squeaks and whistles, winding up into a cacophony of musical notes any percussion section would have been proud of. The wind section buffeted towards a crescendo, which erupted into a trumpeting fanfare of an explosion that rippled odiously through the bedclothes.

By then, the hot chocolate had filtered down to my bladder. I needed to go to the loo, but I was too settled to move. Mind and body began a battle. 'Hold on, it is only another three hours until you get up,' pleaded my brain. 'I've got to go,' cried my bladder. Bladder won. I swung out of bed, staggered down the landing and switched on the bathroom light. This was an act of sheer cruelty to my eyeballs, as the intense brightness sent them whizzing around in my sockets so I couldn't see properly. I groped for the toilet lid, pulled it up and plonked my bottom on the cold, plastic seat. If I had been anywhere near getting to sleep, the sudden chill on my rear end put all that into reverse. I was now wide awake.

Suitable emptied, I climbed back into bed. It was getting light. The local birds (feathered variety) were tuning up for their dawn chorus. A pigeon began cooing on my roof, non-stop. I pulled the blanket up over my head to try and block out the noise. Two minutes later, I threw it off, because I was too hot. Two minutes later, I pulled it up again, because I was getting chilled by the freshening morning air. Commuter traffic was now building up on the nearby motorway. I looked at the clock; there was an hour and a half before I needed to get up for work. I could surely cram in ninety minutes of quality sleep.

The alarm rang, ruining my passionate embrace with Brad Pitt. I thought, 'I'll give it five more minutes before I get up.' Forty five minutes later, Jackie woke me up. I leapt out of bed and had to skip my breakfast, so I could get to work on time, dropping Jackie off at college along the way. But, somewhere in my jumbled night's sleep, an idea had formed. We might be able to find a way forward.

As a last hope I turned to David Allan, a whiz kid of an accountant I used when I had a business. I wrote him a long letter setting out the facts, and he replied:-

"I think that you need some specialist advice from a mortgage broker to see whether it is possible to re-mortgage the property.....you might be eligible for an interest only mortgage until you die. The situation is difficult, but not impossible...."

At last, a glimmer of hope.

I was introduced David Gamester, a consultant at Arnott Guy and Company, independent investment and pension consultants. My income from the three jobs was considered more than enough to cover any new mortgage, my age was possibly a problem, but young David was brilliant at pulling rabbits out of hats and extracting new mortgages out of building societies for senior citizens. He confessed that sorting me out would be 'a challenge,' but a few days after we met he'd almost got everything in place. He had secured a fifteen year interest only mortgage with The Woolwich, a discount package of 1.96% over two years, free valuation, free legal fees package, and no administration fee payable. And the monthly repayments at that time were half of that I had been paying to The Alliance and Leicester. And for all that, his bill to me was only £150.00.

My stress levels plummeted. Jackie was smiling again. All I had to do now was to hand over the £30, 180.74 and I could then apply to have the bankruptcy annulled. It would be history, leaving not a blemish on my credit records.

But legal matters work slowly. A sheaf of correspondence passed around between me, the trustees, my solicitor and The Woolwich's solicitor, dragging out the situation. I just wanted it to be all done and dusted. Files got lost, professionals handling the case went on holidays, but by July 2002 Wynn Baxter, the business recovery group, sent me a welcome letter.

> *"Please find copy of Notice of Final Meeting of your Creditors. This is to obtain my release as Trustee. .....I have now distributed to all creditors who proved in your bankruptcy 100p in the pound with full statutory interest........However, as you have paid your creditors in full, you are entitled to have your bankruptcy annulled. This will ensure that your bankruptcy status is cancelled. ....You would have to make an application to Eastbourne County court serving a copy of your application on both the Official Receiver and myself when it is listed for hearing. I would then simply prepare an affidavit stating that you had paid all your debts in full, submit that to the Court and your annulment would be fairly straightforward."*

On the 27th August 2002 the meeting was held, and in November the Trustee's file was closed. With the Certificate of Discharge came a cheque for £772.54 which was the amount remaining in the account after everyone had been paid. Now all I had to do was go for the annulment.

So in April 2003 there began another round of legal documents, using enough paper to decimate a large section of Amazon rain forest. The Land Registry would be able to remove the charge on my house, so I could now sell it, if I wished to. Documents had to be lodged at Court, showing that all the debts had been paid. This dragged on until September. I had to sign a statement of truth, confirming all my creditors had been paid in full, and 'respectfully ask that the said Bankruptcy Order be annulled and the petition be dismissed.' By November all the necessary documents were gathered together and on the 13th January 2004 at 10am, I found myself again sitting behind the same large shiny table in the County Law Courts. Facing me was Mr. District Judge Robinson, who scanned the paperwork and nodded his head.

"Fine," he said, "We can go ahead with this."

I didn't need a tissue this time; instead I could have leant over and kissed him.

"Thank you so much," I said, feeling so jubilant I couldn't stop grinning as I walked out, clutching form 6.71. Order of Annulment Under Section 282 of the Insolvency Act 1986.

> *"......It is ordered that the Bankruptcy Order dated 11th November 1992 against Miss Elizabeth Ann Wright is hereby annulled...And it is ordered that the petition filed on the 11th November 1992 be dismissed."*

The slate had been wiped clean, it had cost me £30,000 and an extra fifteen years of mortgage, but the house was mine again, a legacy that I could pass onto Jackie.

We went out for a celebratory dinner, talked, laughed and got merry. The future seemed bright.

The next evening I bounced into work at the warehouse, ready to do my evening stint. Everyone was looking glum.

"What's wrong?"

"The company is closing down this branch of the business for economic reasons; we're all shortly going to be out of our jobs."

The Cosmetic Factory

The advertisement looked interesting:-

"WANTED – line operatives for evening work in a cosmetics factory."

The interview was cursory; I'd got another job, from 6pm until 10pm, with a much-needed additional wage packet again.

On my first evening, as I drove into the factory car park, I felt that the depressingly big, grey concrete building bore a passing resemblance to a crematorium. A notice on the main gate said, "WARNING. This area is patrolled by guard dogs." Underneath someone had added, "Dog bites first, asks questions afterwards."

I negotiated my way carefully through an assortment of clapped-out old bangers, motor-bikes and bicycles and followed a group of workers through a door which led into a staff canteen. Some twenty people were sat at tables, talking, eating and drinking. I approached the nearest person,

"I'm new here. Can you point me in the direction of Molly, please? She's going to show me around."

They shouted across the room to a red-head whose hair colour owed more to science in a bottle than nature. "Oi, Molly, someone's looking for you, says you're going to show them around this dump."

As Molly came over, a worker called out, "How did you get on with your date last night?" Mollie replied, "Awful. Bit like my microwave, finished in 30 seconds." Another voice said, "But it wasn't a cooked meal you were after, was it Molly?" The canteen erupted with laughter.

Molly turned to me, "Ignore that lot. Come on, I'll show you the ropes."

She took me into the supply room where the shelves were filled with factory clothing and equipment.

"New employee for kitting out."

A large lady with long blonde pigtails bobbed up from behind the wooden counter.

"Right, what dress and shoe size?"

"Oh, sixteen and six."

She quickly made a selection from the stock, and plonked it down in front of me.

"Here you are. Shoes, hairnet, overall, ear plugs, goggles and protective gloves." She paused, adding with a smile – "Condoms, morning after pill, appointment at the AIDS clinic."

The heavy duty shoes made Doc Martins look like ballet pumps, the overall had buttons missing off the front, and the goggles were apparently to prevent me being blinded by bottles that would occasionally torpedo off the fast moving production line.

When we reached the filling section of the factory floor I could only look on in horror. Rows of moving conveyor belts were noisily passing through assorted pieces of equipment, with tatty chairs set along their lengths. Music from the local radio station was blaring out over the intercom system. The machinery, in various stages of disrepair and decay, was making hideous mechanical grinding sounds. Everyone was shouting. Ear plugs were going to be essential.

Molly yelled, "You'll be working on this line." She indicated the nearest one. "State of the art technology here, well it was in 1945. What do you want to do? Bonk, screw or strip, not necessarily in that order."

I swallowed nervously. "Well, er...."

She carried on, "As you're new we'll put you on the end of the line. It's an easy job, just check the bottles that come through, see they are full, that the lids are on tight and the labels are on straight. Then chuck 'em in these cardboard boxes, twelve at a time. Shut the lid and push the cartons through here." She indicated towards a dragon's mouth of a contraption holding large rolls of sticky tape.

"This will seal the boxes and they'll then pass along a conveyor belt to the warehouse for dispatch. It couldn't be easier."

I had to ask, "What if anything goes wrong?"

"Oh, just bang that red emergency button and everything will come to a stop. No problem."

I took one of the made up boxes and placed it in front of me. Molly went to the head of the line and sat down. Other workers took their places. A voice shouted, "Everyone ready?" Molly pressed a button, a bell rang, the machinery moaned and reluctantly began to operate. A steady stream of bottled baby oil progressed down the conveyor belt, moving threateningly towards me like an advancing army. I braced myself and grabbed the first bottles, checking them as quickly as possible for faults, before placing them in the box. Having closed the lid, I went to push it through the sealing machine, not realising that it had a nasty habit of grabbing the cartons. The box was snatched from my grasp, sealed and swiftly spewed out the other end, gliding onto the conveyor belt and whisked away to the warehouse.

I watched it go, pleased that I'd got the system right, only to turn around and find the baby oil bottles were whizzing towards me and stacking up at an alarming rate. At this speed I could only give each one a cursory glance before tossing it into the container. But I was not going fast enough. As I hastily pushed the next box through the sealer, it grabbed my arm and swiftly wound sticky tape around my limb. I was trapped, and no- one had noticed because they were all engaged in earnest conversations.

More bottles nudged down the end of the line, but there was no more room for them. They began toppling off and smashing on the floor. The sticky tape was holding onto my arm as firmly as a pit bull terrier, I couldn't reach the red button. More bottles slid off the end. There was an ever-widening, slippery pool of oil on the floor.

I eventually managed to wrestle myself free and, holding an open box at the end of the line, just let the bottles fall in. But the sealing machine then had a nervous breakdown and stuck itself together, so I couldn't push anything through. I punched the red button. Nothing happened. The steady march of bottles continued, the music blared, conversations carried on. I started shouting, but my cries of "Stop, stop," were lost in the cacophony of noise. I frantically punched the button again as another dozen bottles hit the concrete. Still nothing. As the puddle of grease grew, I started to slide around like a demented ice-skater. I punched the button with all my might. This time it worked. Everything came to a stop. Everyone looked in my direction as, sheepishly, I emerged from under the conveyor belt, covered in sticky tape and baby oil.

All I could think of to say was, "Sorry, what were those instructions again?"

Most of the line errors, wonky labels, badly fitting tops, and misshapen bottles ended up in the factory shop. Here employees could buy these products for 10p each, limited to ten each per week. Hair shampoos proved to be popular, followed by body creams and foot care products. One of the fastest movers were bottles labelled 'Ladies-for intimate body use,' about which Molly laughingly said, "I don't know what it does for your fanny, but, by golly, it's brilliant stuff for cleaning windows."

But human nature being what it was, a number of the shop customers couldn't count and would emerge clutching carrier bags overflowing with products, which they flogged off to friends, neighbours and at boot sales. One enterprising senior member of the team found out where the shop key was hidden, and, when he thought no-one was looking, used to reverse his car up to the back door and fill the boot with dozens of bottles. Management eventually got to hear about the fast disappearing 'seconds' and security was tightened up. But this didn't stop alternative dubious acquisition of the products.

As the bottles progressed down each line, a few never reached the end. Along the way, they were re-directed into the volumous pockets of the women's overalls. Those that had started the evening with bikini shaped figures, ended up waddling to the ladies changing room looking like busty Boudicca's in advanced pregnancy.

A number of the one hundred and twenty employees were agency workers, brought in to help out when necessary. We had a mixture of nationalities, Portuguese, Spanish, Russian and French. Most were transient, we saw them only once and they were gone. If there was an extra large order to complete, some might stay for a couple of weeks.

During one such session, Bill sat opposite me. We were putting the caps on hair shampoo bottles by hand, before they disappeared into a 'screwing' machine that tightened them up. Bill always turned up in a vest and khaki shorts, both of which had seen better days. He often used to sit next to Adam, who appeared to have a nervous twitch, which was not ideally suited to a moving, precision orientated production line, when it wasn't having one of its mechanical mishaps.

When the starting bell rang, the conveyor belt would groan into action and we would begin to put on the caps. It was a boring routine, occasionally interrupted by bits of the machinery breaking down, falling off or completely screwing up. We would chat loudly amongst ourselves, talking about everyday things to pass the time. I noticed that Bill was using only one hand to put the occasional cap on the passing bottles. The other one was down his nether regions, either re-arranging his male anatomy or indulging in pocket billiards. Adam was watching him and started to violently twitch, causing his handful of caps to shoot across the floor.

Health and safety had decreed that items strewn on the floor have to be quickly picked up as they constituted a hazard to anyone walking by. The line was stopped as Molly said, "What on earth are you doing, throwing them on the floor?"

Adam squirmed in his seat.

"I didn't do it," he protested.

"Yes you did, I saw you."

"I didn't."

"Well, pick them up and let's get on."

He crawled around retrieving the caps and sat down. Bill was grinning.

The line restarted and after a short time Bill's hand went down the front of his trousers again. Adam twitched violently and a dozen more caps whizzed across the factory floor. But before anyone could do or say anything, the screwing machine ground to a halt. A number of bottles had spun into the guts of the machine, jamming the system.

Stan, the line manager, whose job it was to oversee employees and nurse our aged line along, went to find his tool box. Occasionally it took unorthodox skills rather than tools to sort out mechanical problems and, this time, a long stick proved more effective than spanners and screwdrivers. The bottles were successfully poked out from where they were playing 'hide and seek,' Adam retrieved his caps, Bill got both hands back into industrial action and the line creaked and cranked up again.

But the screwing machine wanted to play games; it then

decided to start throwing the bottles out the other end. Like guided missiles they hurtled towards unsuspecting employees, sitting targets in their chairs further down the line. Hit by flying containers of hair shampoo, they fled, nursing their bruises.

The line was closed for a proper repair and we were integrated into the team filling up squat bottles of creamy hair gel. The main machine discharged a white concoction of froth from a clear dustbin sized container; the bottles were then capped by hand, passed through 'the bonker,' which bashed the caps on tight, then the conveyor belt took them onto the section where labels were wrapped around and sealed. But we must have bought our jinx with us. Within minutes the hair gel dispenser went into overdrive, squirting out white foam at an alarming rate. It rapidly filled up its protective case, and then the lotion started to bubble over the top, run down the sides and drip on the floor. This was a scene from Dr. Who and an alien invasion, as the white mass crept menacingly along the concrete. The red alarm button was having another one of its bad days, and wouldn't turn off. A thump with one of Stan's hammers finally did the trick. We spent the rest of the evening with buckets and cloths trying to mop up the mess.

Next day our production line was back to normal, but the agency had sent a new team of workers. Opposite me sat Mohammed and Joe, or Little and Large, as I wanted to call them. Mohammed was a small guy, less than five feet, with a neat black beard and bushy eyebrows. Joe was a hunky black man, with rippling muscles throughout his large frame. I smiled and said, "Hi," but they just looked back and said nothing. They performed the tasks as they were told, stuck together like glue and apparently didn't want to socialise. At tea break they sat at a table by themselves, always engaged in earnest conversations. By the fourth day Mohammed had thawed a little, holding

162

out my chair for me to sit on. "Thank you," I said, he simply smiled and gave a little nod. He passed bundles of caps to me, saving me from delving into the dispenser.

"I think he fancies you," said Molly, who had a one-track mind.

"Don't be daft, he's just being polite and helpful," I replied, "Besides he's probably a Muslim, he wouldn't be allowed to start anything other than with someone of his religion."

As the days went by, Mohammed's gentlemanly actions continued, carried out with politeness and small head nods. He and Joe appeared to have little grasp of the English language, so it was impossible to engage them in any sort of conversation. I felt touched that Mohammed should be so caring. A lot of the male workers would push you out of the way to get to the most comfortable chairs on the production line; it was refreshing to find a man who personally selected a seat and carefully held it out for me to sit upon. I tried to start conversations but he just gave a suggestion of a smile and waved his hands in a dismissive way. I presumed he couldn't understand me. I felt flattered.

On the tenth day neither he nor Joe turned up. I knew they had been engaged for a long haul, there were large overseas orders to fulfil.

"What's happened to Joe and Mohammed?" I asked Molly. She was the usual source of gossip and information. She looked flustered and replied, "I don't know." It was obvious she did know, but wasn't saying. Two young students sat in their chairs, and I was back to hustling out my own seat.

Reading the local paper a few days later the headlines screamed out about 'Terrorists being found in the town.' Joe and Mohammed were part of a gang living in a multi-occupation house where they had been organising devastation for areas of the country and London in particular. Bomb making equipment was found. They had been arrested and taken away. Finding work through an agency had given them an acceptable cover for their evil operations. I was just glad that there hadn't been a role reversal in those two seats opposite. If Adam with his twitch, and Bill with his perchance for squeezing balls had been the terrorists instead, half of southern England would have been blown up.

Coming in one Monday evening, we all noticed that the hair gel production line had been taken away. "Gone to one of our other factories in Poland," we were told. The big supermarkets, the company's best customers, had started a round of price reductions, trying to outdo each other to gain more customers. The knock-on effect was lower payments for the goods, and staff reductions. More machinery was moved out. Staff numbers were reduced. The inevitable happened, we could see it coming. The company was moving completely to Poland, where costs were far less. In six months we would all be out of a job. There was the usual talk of negotiation and unions; help was offered from recruitment agencies. Economists put in their two-penny worth, but they were the sort of people who would spend their time rearranging the chairs on the Titanic. But as I left after the party on the last day, all I could think of was "Bloody hell, here we go again. I'm left holding the parcel when the music stops."

The Vacuum Cleaner

The vacuum cleaner that I'd found in a skip a long time ago, had served me well. But, it finally hit metallic meltdown and stopped working. I changed the fuse, hoping this might solve the problem, but the machine had definitely died. So I went down to the retail store to see what was on offer in the lower price range.

I just wanted a basic upright one that was capable of keeping the carpets looking ok. Here there were dozens on view; red round ones with smiley faces, with 'Henry' or 'James' written above their eyebrows. I passed on these; I wasn't looking for a metal friend, just an efficient piece of machinery. Displayed alongside were large uprights with ugly gargantuan protuberances that wouldn't have been out of place booming, "Exterminate, exterminate," as they zoomed around a Dr. Who TV programme. There were squat little things in pale pinks, blues and purples that didn't appear big enough to be capable of sucking up bits from carpets.

The sales rep. had a short piece of dusty carpet at the ready for a practical demonstration. He sprinkled some dust mixed with garden compost all over it, and said, "Would Madam like to see a machine in action?" He smiled, his teeth doing a great display of advertising a tooth whitening product. I was tempted to say, 'No, just looking' and walk away, leaving him standing with his dusty pile.

The dazzling smile went off his face when I said, "I just want the cheapest upright vacuum cleaner you've got. Nothing fancy."

He pulled a demonstration model out from the line up, "How will this one do, its £49.99."

It seemed to suck up the rubbish by his feet in an efficient way, so I was convinced this would do for me and paid up. He fetched me a brand new boxed vacuum cleaner from the back of the shop, handed it over with another dazzling smile, and moved on to the next customers.

Once home, the colourful square box looked positively inviting. It wasn't heavy, had a nice simple picture on the front and it didn't need an ultra - sharp, heavy duty kitchen knife to undo the wrapping. Lulled into a false sense of satisfaction, I opened the lid. The first challenge was trying to extract the product from amongst the chunks of unyielding cardboard, bubble wrap and plastic bags. The second obstacle was trying to put it together.

As usual, the instruction manual was printed in about 100 different languages, backed up by dodgy line drawings of the front and back views of the machine. There were twenty-two points of note, from where to put the crevice tool to locating the lower hose inspection pipe.

After a page of safety instructions filled with grim warnings not to stick your fingers into the electrical bits when plugged in, I got to the 'How to Assemble' page, which added, ominously, 'some parts may vary according to the model.' And they did. Faced with 'Firmly push the back panel onto the base assembly,' I hadn't a clue what this mysterious and unidentified part was. The picture was unhelpful, just a simple, brief sketch with a thick black arrow pointing at some squiggles. By a lengthy process of elimination, I finally found the back base and shoved it in. 'Slide the handle into place onto the top of the back panel and secure the top handle to the back panel by inserting the two long screws.' These two items came in a plastic bag big enough to hold a week's shopping.

But the handle stubbornly refused to be slid into place so I could match up the screw holes. There was no mention in the assembly manual of any standby tools, so I got a big hammer from my tool box and gave the offending item a couple of satisfying thumps. The screws slid in a treat.

The instructions then got more mysterious, the drawings less understandable. 'Insert the bottom of the dirt container to align with the tab on the upper cover of the motor. To secure the dirt container, push the top in place.' But, when I pushed the bottom in place, the top didn't fit, if I pushed in at the top, the bottom base stuck out. Out came the hammer again.

I found that the colour picture on the front of the box more helpful than the instruction booklet, and all the pieces that I'd laid out on the carpet eventually found a home.

Back to the manual it said, 'This vacuum cleaner is equipped with a convenient cord storage feature.'- (Two small plastic hooks.)

'The bottom cord holder has a quick release.'- (Rotate the bottom hook and all the cable spills off onto the floor.)

There was far more cable than the hooks could cope with, it kept spilling off, and once into intertwined overload, I was in danger of instant electrocution as it rolled dangerously under the machine.

Having taken note of the WARNING – 'To avoid injury, keep loose clothing, hair, fingers and all other parts of the body away from any moving parts (such as the brushes)' – I was a little nervous about starting up this mini-monster. I took a deep breath, stamped on the red switch and the motor roared into life. With its dynamic engine the sucking power was a sight to behold. The carpets were almost dragged up from the floor, and like a lion at a kill, this machine was not going to give up its prey easily. It viciously and noisily held onto a chunk of the woollen material, defying me to pull it out.

And, where air is drawn in, it must come out. A forceful jet stream erupted from somewhere at the top of the dust cylinder, so powerful it promptly blew all the ornaments off the mantelpiece and my neat pile of newspapers, stacked ready for the recycling bin, were whisked away through an open window by this aerated eruption and were never seen again.

In no time at all the bag - less cylinder had filled up with an amazing assortment of fluffy detritus sucked out of my carpets by this efficient 1600 motor. Taking it all apart for emptying was easy, putting the parts back again was not. The hammer had another outing.

Then Sadie phoned, "Can I have a quick borrow of your vacuum cleaner, mine's just died on me and I've got visitors coming."

"Of course, you can, I'll pop it in the car and bring it around shortly."

She'd moved into temporary accommodation whilst her landlord was arranging to have her house underpinned, as it had mysteriously started to subside into an ever widening system of small tunnels. She, and all her pets, were now living nearer to me, in a small house sited at the top of a steep hill.

As I laid the vacuum cleaner on the back seat of my car, I noticed there was a strong breeze blowing. By the time I'd reached Sadie's home this had turned into a gale force wind, which grabbed at my car door, threatening to wrench it off its hinges. I carefully stood the vacuum cleaner down in the road and vainly tried to get the door shut. An ever stronger gust of wind suddenly snatched at the appliance; it started to move, and before I could catch it, a car driver coming up the hill was confronted by the bizarre sight of an unaccompanied upright vacuum cleaner freewheeling down the hill. Aided by another blast of air, it gathered more speed, shot around a bend, and as I arrived, it had run into someone's driveway, smashed into a sturdy tree, scattering more parts around than were in the original box.

Job Hunting, Again

So, clutching my P45 I started looking for another job to help pay off the mortgage. But being in my sixties, searching for the Holy Grail would have been easier. Previously there was never a problem finding employment; so I enthusiastically told prospective employers that 'sixty was the new forty', but in their eyes I was past it.

I thoroughly perused a stack of job related paperwork laid out in front of me. Computer technician? – No, my computer knowledge was practically nil. Certified aborist? – Well, Jackie was always telling me that I was so scatty I probably needed certifying. Cook? – Charcoal maker would be a more appropriate title for my culinary skills. Cleaner? – I'm from the school of 'As long as it looks ok on the surface, just don't run your finger along the top of the wardrobe. You could probably write a mini War and Peace up there.' Sandwich delivery driver? – Not when the hours start at 7.30 am. I'd barely gone to bed by that time.

There was the good old standby – shelf stacking. I did a trawl around the supermarkets, asking for job application forms, which in some cases turned out to be as thick as paperback books. Most of the staff at the public relations counters handed out the forms with a cheerful attitude and a sympathetic smile, probably thinking 'poor old soul, can't survive on her pension.' One assistant looked down her nose at me, as if I had come in with something nasty stuck to the bottom of my shoe, sniffed loudly and said in a superior and dismissive voice , 'we don't take on any extra staff until Easter.'

Even for a shelf stacking job, there were page of lengthy questions.

'What do you think you can bring to this job?'

I was tempted to reply, 'Me. All twelve and a half stone of me. The extra half stone being because I pigged out over Christmas.' What did they want to know? I didn't need a university degree to place items on shelves. I'd got all my marbles and a pair of hands to do that type of work.

'Sex?' I was tempted to put 'Oh, yes please, and plenty of it,' but noticed that most other forms had grappled with too many saucy answers and substituted 'gender' for 'sex'.

'Why are you applying for this position?'

Silly question, it was obvious, for the money.

'What are you salary expectations?' Salary? Must be the wrong form.

Whatever I wrote, I would end up with the basic wage.

'How would you ensure that we put our customers first?'

This was where I didn't tell them of my shortfall in purchaser care in a pet shop when a customer regularly let her randy, territory marking, male dog pee all over the floor. She was astonished when I finally complained about the mess and stormed out after I had produced a bucket and mop and made her clear it up.

But eventually a couple of prospective employers took their chances on my rapidly improving skills at application form filling and asked me in for interviews. The first was with a pie maker, way out in the country, which did a daily round of farmer's markets, selling his tasty wares from a stall. Work started at 6am, which was not my favourite time. But I was getting financially desperate and decided that I just needed to re-arrange my social life to get my eight hours 'beauty sleep.' In depth questioning about my abilities to drive a battered 4 x 4 pulling a fully loaded trailer, erect a tent, hump sandbags to hold it down in gales, and display the home cooked foods, made me realise that I should have donned wellies and an anorak, instead of a smart black jacket and skirt. I didn't get the job, but came away with a fantastically flavoured, hot steak pie that helped out with the food bill for a week.

Interviews for the other job, where staff were required for the opening of a new house-furnishing store, were held in the plush surroundings of the Job Centre. On entering, I was overwhelmingly impressed by the thick blue carpet, clean air, gentle music and quiet atmosphere, overseen by a polite and helpful doorman, who doubled up as a bouncer to troublemakers. This was so far removed from my previous experiences of such a place, where I'd had to peruse and select cards listing jobs from wooden A stands. These I then took to a suitable desk, wending my way nervously through a line of weary, often smelly, cigarette-smoking individuals waiting for their dole money. Many were argumentatively drunk and their frequent and noisy ejections out of the boarded-up front door were a satisfying spectator sport.

Here, there were comfy chairs that I could have fallen asleep in. The interviews were being held in two glass-screened rooms. Forty minutes later I emerged into the sunlight having answered endless, detailed questions about my ability to work as part of a team, cope with customers, what my hobbies and interests were, and where would I like to see myself in the company in ten years time? I slid around that one, as 'probably pushing up daisies' didn't seem to be the answer they were looking for.

Sure enough, two weeks later, a postcard plopped through the letter-box, thwarting my hopes yet again. 'Thank you for attending the interview, but I regret to inform you that we feel you were not quite right for us, but we wish you luck in your job search.'

Yes, you and me both.

Becoming A Writer

"I think I've found an easy way to earn a living," I said to Jackie as we sat in the busy dentist's waiting room. As we tried to shut out the unnerving whirr and screech of his drill, I showed her some of the magazines laid out on the table. A few were rather ancient and dog-eared, but in them I thought I'd struck publishing gold.

"I've been reading some of these short stories whilst we've been waiting, and I know I can write better ones. See here, they say they are paying upwards of one hundred pounds for each one published. Well, I could easily turn out.....say, two or three a week." My self confidence was unencumbered by doubt.

Cynically, Jackie raised her eyes to heaven and said, "Oh yes, right."

"Of course I can, it's got to be so easy, making up stories, writing them down, sending them off and waiting for the lovely cheques to arrive."

"Mum, I don't think it is as simple as that, everyone would be doing it otherwise."

The screeching drill stopped. You could have heard a cockroach fart in the ensuing five second silence. Then the buzz of conversation started up again, peppered with nervous giggles and laughs. Obviously no-one wanted to be here, but the demands of good oral hygiene put bums on dentist's chairs.

Emerging half an hour later, relieved we had both escaped fillings, just been given a good check up and clean, I expanded on my idea.

"I've got lots of ideas for stories, it's surely worth a try and it's not going to cost much, just the postage."

"Well, if you want to do it, go ahead," Jackie said, on her way for an evening out with her friends.

I knew stored somewhere in the house was an old

manual typewriter I had rescued from a skip a few years ago. I hunted everywhere for it, ending my search in the cupboard under the stairs. As I moved around aged suitcases containing family memorabilia, old pictures in wobbly frames that had never got hung, shoes and clothes I never wore, to children's toys Jackie had long grown out of, I couldn't work out how I had managed to cram it all into such a small space. Just when I had almost given up, I found the typewriter. Although dust laden and home to a few spiders, it scrubbed up nicely with the help of a damp cloth.

I sneakily tore a few pages out of the back of one of Jackie's college exercise books and, teasing one onto the roller, gave it a firm turn before pressing a couple of keys. The print was faint, and the letters e and r came out entwined, but I bashed away with two fingers, finishing a story that appeared to be from the viewpoint of an 'on the tiles cat' but turns out to be a man. Magazines seemed to like these stories with a 'twist in the tail.' I tore out a few more pages and carried on typing.

By the time Jackie came home I had produced six stories that I was exceedingly pleased with. The print had faded to near unreadable, mistakes covered up with dollops of Tippex, but I felt that editors, when they had read my masterpieces, could tolerate these small imperfections.

Now all I had to do was to find suitable markets. This wasn't a problem, as I had picked out six of the leading women's magazines. I sent one to each, telling them how good my stories were and I could supply them with plenty more. I enclosed stamped addressed envelopes for speedy replies. The outgoing brown envelopes dropped into the post box with a satisfying thump, and I walked home on cloud nine, positive that my dream of a far better income was just around the corner.

I eagerly watched for the postman during the next

few days. Flyers, bills and free offers were speedily discarded in my search for editors' replies. Days dragged into a week, one week into two weeks, until I saw one of my returned envelopes on the doormat. I snatched it up, tore it open, wildly expecting, at the very least, to see a contract to supply dozens of stories over the next few years, plus a cheque for the one they had.

The photocopied reply was brief – "Sorry, this isn't quite for us. Herewith returned." There wasn't even a signature. A standard rejection slip that was joined by five more during the next few days.

"Look at that," I said angrily to Jackie, "These editors just don't know talent when they see it."

"Well mum, I did say I didn't think it was going to be that easy."

"In that case, I'll find six other markets; someone out there must think my stories are brilliant."

Off went another half a dozen brown envelopes, days later back came half a dozen brown envelopes enclosing varying polite rejections. I was furious that no one had spotted what gems my short stories were. I laid them out on the table and had a re-read of the contents. Perhaps they weren't quite as good as I had thought; maybe they needed a few alterations.

I spotted an advertisement in a newspaper – "Why not be a Writer?"

This offered a home study creative writing course containing all I needed to know to become a wealthy, published writer. There were pictures of successful students earning four and five figure sums after completing the course. There was a fifteen day free trial, and the promise of a full refund guarantee that if I didn't make more than the cost of the course fees by the time I had completed it.

My only stumbling block was finding the money to pay for the tuition. I wrote and said that I would love to be a writer and would they like to take the cost of my fees from out of my first published successes. To my great disappointment, they declined; the money had to be paid up front, so I juggled around with my finances to stump up the three figure sum.

When the big blue box containing all the instruction booklets arrived, I spent days poring over the contents. I learnt a lot. I bought proper A4 copier paper; a friend, who was upgrading, offered me a word processor and printer, complete with user's manual the size of a block-buster book, so out went the Tippex and old typewriter. After a couple of hour's tuition I was ready to tackle the world. Mistakes could be erased at the touch of a button, whole paragraphs could be moved around. The elderly printer, of daisy wheel design, reluctantly disgorged pristine printed sheets, accompanied by clacking noises so loud that my neighbours began to think I was running evening tap dancing classes.

I learnt from my tutor that, as a newcomer to writing, I had to start at the bottom. Publication would be more likely if I began with a few letters, possibly topical, to local newspapers or magazines. The first, satisfying small success came when one of my submissions was accepted by a women's magazine. Just an observation on life.

"Although I have been driving for a number of years, I am still rubbish at reversing. Taking a non-driving friend out to do some shopping at the local supermarket, I cruised around the busy car park, desperately looking for a parking space.

Seeing some vehicular movement in the next lane, I dashed around just as two cars pulled out. Carefully lining up, I put my car into reverse and backed in.

'Oh, aren't you good at this,' said my friend as we got out. I hadn't the heart to tell her I'd actually been aiming for the adjacent parking spot."

This was followed by a cheque for £10. I was on my way to my first million.

Encouraged at seeing my name in print, I rashly churned out reams of letters on any subject I could think of. They disappeared down editorial black holes.

In spite of all my efforts to save it with a number of metal transplants, the word processor eventually crumpled and collapsed under my excessive demands. I gave it a decent send-off at the local re-cycling centre, gently placing it between a rusty lawnmower and a wonky bedstead. The chunky, dog-eared manual was forced between the cavernous mouth of the waste paper bin.

With technology racing ahead by the day, as people upgraded, there were plenty of second-hand computers coming onto the market at knock-down prices. For £50 I got a passingly ok contraption with a smart work station complete with all its feet, a bubble jet printer, flatbed scanner and a comfy office chair.

I had to learn a whole new technical language, as those Windows didn't need cleaning, there were other Rams apart from sheep that said 'Baa' and the Internet was not a useful tool for catching goldfish in the garden pond.

But I floundered in a retro time-warp as I tried to come to terms with modern technology; I was in awe of a machine that, although only made of plastic, silicone chips and assorted wires, appeared to be much smarter than me. It flashed up messages of reprimand, accompanied by attention seeking chimes, when I occasionally hit the wrong keys.

'You have performed an illegal operation!'

No, I haven't, I'm just trying to write a letter, not break into a bank.

Or it thought it was smugly clever, when asked to print something out, by telling me, 'Monochrome cartridge detected!'

Yes, I knew that, I only use black ink.

When I wrote any letters, a hairy little man popped out from behind the margins and asked, 'Do you need help writing this letter?'

No thanks – I could mange perfectly well by myself, and enjoyed taking revenge by clicking the mouse onto the cancel button and zapping him off the screen.

Asked to print out multiple pages of the same copy, the computer threw the odd hissy-fit, and refused, throwing up a warning sign that it was not talking to the printer. Pressing the details button to find out why, I was presented with a screen full of jumbled letters and numbers that made me wonder if my computer was being used as a depository for top secret files from the government's Bletchley Park de-coding base.

Its party piece was to freeze. Nothing moved on the screen. No amount of persuasion could produce any flicker of movement.

"Its crashed," said Jackie, the first time it happened, and, in spite of her best effort at trawling the keyboard with the same kind of speed she reserved for mobile phone texting, it stayed crashed. So we did the ultimate no-no and pulled out the plug, and left it for ten minutes to get its act together again. Once its life support system was restored it had a sulk and annoyingly slowly checked all its bits and pieces for viruses and then double checked that it hadn't been tampered with. I was however, up and running again, ready to start turning out more features that editors wouldn't be able to resist.

Looking for a subject to write about, I noticed that, In the property section of the local paper, there was a lighthouse for sale that had been de-commissioned and turned into a residential home. Belle Tout, is an iconic landmark, situated in an isolated position on the chalk cliffs of Beachy Head.

I turned up some useful information at the local library. This dumpy little tower, made of Aberdeen granite blocks, had been extended and improved over one hundred and eighty years. It had been totally useless as a lighthouse, being situated up too high for its light to be seen through thick sea mists, soon after being decommissioned in 1902 it was purchased from Trinity House by Mr. Davis-Gilbert for £200.

Its history and long survival was fascinating and I felt that if I was finding the information interesting, surely magazine readers would too. I needed to know more. The estate agent could surely be of help. I sat looking at the phone, trying to pluck up courage to contact them. Would this be my big break? I dialled the number. A calm man's voice replied, "Badger and Sons, estate agents, can I help you?"

With fingers crossed behind my back, I answered, "I have been asked by a national magazine to do a feature on Belle Tout lighthouse. Is there any possibility that I could have a chat with the owner to get some background information? Of course I'd be glad to mention your company name at the end of the article."

A pause - 'Please, please say yes,' my whole being willed a positive reply. My financial future depended on it.

"We'll have to discuss this with the seller and we'll phone you back."

The next fifteen minutes seemed the longest in my life. When the phone rang I jumped, my throat had gone so dry I could hardly speak.

"Hello."

"Miss Wright, yes that would be fine. Mr. Castleton will be happy to speak to you on Saturday morning. Just go up to the wrought iron garden gates and ring the security bell."

Jackie came in and caught me dancing around the room.

"What's the matter with you?"

"I've just got an appointment for my first article interview, up at the lighthouse."

"Oh," she said, "I thought it was something really exciting."

The seats in the local library were well sat upon during the next few days as I perused books for more background facts. I made a list of questions to ask Mr. Castleton, this information filled feature was going to knock the socks off some lucky editor. Then I realised it might sell better if there were some photographs to accompany it. Only I didn't own a camera.

But I knew a man who did. Marion, who'd worked with me at David's pet shop, had a partner, Bob, who was a wizard with a camera. Could he help out?

"Of course, I can, this sounds fascinating," came the welcome reply.

At the appointed time on Saturday, we drove up to the top of Beachy Head cliffs, which was shrouded in an unseasonable thick mist. As we walked up the steep access road, the lighthouse emerged from the gloom looking like some giant chess piece. Having rung the bell by the garden gate, Mr. Castleton let us in and made us welcome.

Out came Bob's camera as he, with the eye of seasoned snapper, saw photographic promise in the quaint architecture, displayed artefacts gleaned from beach shipwrecks, and colourful rooms with seafaring themes. Smiling happily, he drifted away, so Mr. Castleton and I settled down to talk. Out came my list of questions, to which he replied with gusto. As valuable bits of information whizzed past my ears, I sat there like a nerd with my little pad and pen, having suddenly realised that, not knowing any shorthand, I couldn't keep up with his speedy verbals. I should have thought things through properly and bought a tape recorder. I struggled to jot down as many relevant facts as I could in my personal version of shorthand, wanting to capture every aspect of this fascinating interview.

Later, as we stood on the tower balcony, now bathed in bright sunlight, I had to ask the obvious question, "Why did you buy Belle Tout?" The answer came as no surprise.

"Take a good look around you. That's why we bought it."

From our elevated position 334 feet above sea level our eyes feasted on spectacular views. To the west, the remains of a Bronze Age settlement and the green trimmed undulations of the 'Seven Sisters' chalk cliffs stretching along the coast to Seaford Head. Eastwards, the high headland of Beachy Head towered over the red and white striped column of the other, more famous lighthouse, on the beach.

Northwards were Kipling's 'blunt, bow-headed, whale-backed downs' and seawards, 30 miles of uninterrupted views across the English channel. The only sounds were the gentle splashing of waves on the beach far below and the songs of skylarks mingling with the mewing of gulls.

Apart from walkers on the nearby South Downs Way, their only other neighbours were rabbits and sheep, and according to local legend, the odd ghost or two.

Breathing in the salty tang carried on the warm breeze, I fell in love with this unique, old lighthouse. If I had lots of money I would have bought it on the spot.

As it was, coming back to reality, I had to go home and write my first 'proper' feature.

"How did you get on with the pictures?" I asked Bob.

"Brilliant, it's such a lovely place, just cried out to be photographed," he replied.

At home, the blank computer screen stared back at me. I didn't know where to start, how to begin that vital, eye-catching opening sentence. Writer's block engulfed me as my brain went dead. The squiggles and jottings in my notebook had been sorted out, making some kind of sense, but were hard to translate to the screen.

Then, out it spilled-

'Imagine owning a cliff top home that is unique; a home that has spectacular views of the Sussex coastline and rolling downs. Where your only neighbours are seagulls, rabbits, sheep and the occasional backpacker trekking along the ancient South Downs Way.' ....

A thousand words later, it was finished. As advised by my course tutor, I put the printed-out article away, distancing myself from the feature. In a few days I could come back and do some ruthless editing.

Next, there was a market to find. Hunting through 'The Writer's and Artist's Year Book,' I narrowed my choice down to a local publication, "Sussex Life."

Composing a query letter, asking if they were interested in my article, took me almost as much time as writing the feature itself. I pushed a stamped addressed envelope in with the letter and popped it all into the post box.

Patience was the name of the game. Magazine editors are busy people, replies take time. I couldn't wait for an answer.

"Get on with the next article," advised my tutor, but I couldn't get my head around anything else. Belle Tout was my first 'baby,' I had to get this one delivered, before I could concentrate on any more.

Days went by, I lost heart, maybe writing wasn't for me. Then the letter box clanged one morning and there laid my returned brown envelope, nestling amongst the brightly coloured, junk mail.

"Aren't you going to pick it up?" enquired Jackie, "You've been waiting days for an answer."

"They might have said 'no thanks' and all my efforts have been wasted."

"Well, open it then and find out."

"It'll probably be a no."

"Oh, mother...."

She grabbed the envelope and tore it open.

"Do you want the good news or the bad news?"

"Is there good news?"

"Yes, they want you to submit the article; the bad news is they want it as soon as possible for their next issue."

"It's all written, I can send it off today with Bob's pictures."

"Well, go and do it then, stop flapping about. This is what you wanted, get stuck in."

"I can't believe they really want to buy my feature...."

"Send it off."

Four neat A4 pages plus a couple of Bob's best pictures were carefully tucked into an envelope and posted.

The January issue of "Sussex Life" was due out around Christmas time. Not knowing the exact date, I kept visiting W.H. Smiths, prowling around the aisles, anxiously looking in every magazine section.

And finally, there they were. A pile of copies neatly stacked. I picked one up and started turning the pages. They were a blur, I realised that I'd left my glasses at home and I couldn't see the print. After turning page after page, there was nothing. My heart sank as I got further to the back of the magazine, and then, there was one of Bob's pictures, with the title, in big, readable print, "Where House Hunters have seen the Light" by Elizabeth Wright.

I punched the air in excitement, yelling "Oh, yes," which got me some funny looks from customers and caught the attention of the security guard, who obviously thought there was a mad women on the loose.

I bought six copies of "Sussex Life" and waved them around.

"Look, I'm published, this is my article in here."

Customers edged nervously away, I'd hoped they

would have come rushing over for my autograph, but they seemed disconcertingly wary of my jubilation.

Talk about being up on cloud nine, I was way past that on at least cumulus twenty-two. Charging in the front door, I laid the copies out with a triumphant flourish in front of Jackie.

"There you are, I've done it, I'm published."

"Good for you, mother, that's just great. What are you going to do now?"

"Wait for the cheque to arrive."

Pitching Pictures

Having managed to sell a few more articles I treated myself to a reasonably good second - hand camera; now I could make extra money by providing my own pictures along with the features. Or, maybe, I could try to sell 'stand-alone' snaps. Some popular women's magazines paid good money for cute, amusing or different shots.

In my garden sat Fred, the flower pot man, facing the water feature, which was a grubby plastic urn laid sideways in a tray of green, slimy pebbles. Fred was made of wood, about the size of a new born baby, and had a small, upturned flower pot on his head that was supposed to pass as a hat. His creosoted arms were angled across his chest, and, in the empty stumps that served as hands, he originally held a small potted plant. Just below his two brass eyes there was a long protuberance of a nose, the size of a costly cigar.

I thought that there might be some financial mileage in taking some pictures of Fred, 'having his holiday in Eastbourne,' where I could photograph him in a variety of well known locations.

"Fred, this is your lucky day," I said to him, as I pulled him off his rock. His terracotta hat fell over his eyes. I sat him on the back seat of the car and drove down to the seaside. Being high summer, parking was difficult, but after six attempts, I managed to nudge into a small gap down a side street, only a short walk from the beach.

The town was full of visitors; there was a non-stop succession of cars along the seafront. With Fred held in my arms like a baby and clutching my digital camera, I struggled to get over the road. A kind hearted motorist slowed down and waved me over. I decided to leg it quickly before other drivers lost their patience. As I ran, still clutching Fred to my chest, my rather large bouncing bust knocked his nose off. It fell in the road and rolled away. My picture plans would be ruined without a complete Fred, so I chased after his nose, now bowling merrily along, helped by a frisky wind. I kept thinking, "Oh, please, please, don't let a passing car squash it." Drivers were trying to dodge me, angrily hooting and flashing their lights, as I desperately tried to catch up with Fred's nose

Having finally managed to get alongside this still moving appendage, I tried to bend over and grab it. But, being well into pensionable age, where my muscles and bones don't work that well, or as quickly as they should, I missed it. With all this effort, I lost my grip on Fred, and, as he hit the tarmac, one of his legs fell off.

I desperately gathered up all his loose parts, made apologetic gestures to annoyed drivers, and headed for the beach. I looked around for photographic inspiration from the location. Maybe I could perch Fred on a breakwater, with the old Victorian pier as a backdrop. Shoving his nose well in, and hammering his leg back on with a large pebble, I sat him on one of the chunky upright posts and got my camera out. But the wind had got stronger, Fred wobbled, his badly attached leg dropped onto the shingle by my feet, and unbalanced, he fell backwards, disappearing over the other side of the breakwater.

There was a scream. I tentatively looked over and saw that Fred was laid out on his back on the pebbles, hat at a rakish angle, looking like some old soak that'd passed out. A small child with a bucket and spade was rubbing his head. His father glared at me and told me in no polite terms what I could do with Fred, much of which was anatomically impossible.

I gave up and headed back home. My idea of using Fred as a subject for an amusing snapshot, dissolved, as I put him back by the water feature. That night a number of students from the local college appeared to be in a celebratory mood. After a visit to the local pub, they trawled around the streets, shouting, whistling and singing, playing a bit of footie, and having the occasional swig from a shared bottle of strong cider.

Next morning I found our little wooden Fred had been interfered with. One of the students, with a great sense of humour, had made Fred a 'Blue Peter' mock up deck chair, sat him in it, and his empty hands were now holding a small plastic glass containing some suspiciously yellow liquid. His flower pot hat was tilted at a 'devil may care' angle.

"That's got to be the picture," I excitedly told Jackie, getting the camera out.

Within a few days the 'Peterborough' columns of the Daily Mail had published it, and I could add another success to my ever growing list of acceptances.

I was doubtful about taking on a commission to put together a feature for a bird magazine about Mr. Grim and Mrs. Reaper, a pair of Vultures. But I went ahead and wrote, - 'So here I am, flattened up against the aviary door, camera in one hand, tape recorder in the other, wondering if I'm about to become dinner to a pair of hungry African White – Backed vultures, which are gazing intently at me......the Birds of Prey trainer, laughingly says, 'You would have to be dead before they will come near you. A twitch of a finger or a blink of an eye lid is enough to put them off feeding.' So I hastily snap out of scared mode, which has reduced me to a rigor mortis type stance, and become extremely animated.

'He offers them a nice juicy rabbit carcase, which they both ignore, instead size up my tubby frame with their piercing eyes, obviously looking for larger helpings. I quickly change my movement strategy into the faster phase of 'Riverdance.' ...... I finished with...'they will be joining the spectacular birds of prey flying displays. Their trainer, with a wry sense of humour, is hoping that a local funeral parlour might sponsor them.'

Another bird that I tried to take pictures of for possible publication, but failed, was of a baby blue tit. We found that a pair of tits had taken up residence in our bird box, and when we started to hear tiny cheeps coming from it, the male became aggressively protective of his babies, and sat on the TV aerial, loudly scolding us. He was joined by his mate, who looked as if she could have done with a good top-to-toe makeover, her plumage having become ruffled and ragged sitting on eggs and feeding hungry youngsters.

A wriggling grub was held in her beak. World-weary, she gave me a cursory glance, ignored her still ranting partner, and flew into the box. The male, his authority apparently undermined, stopped his scolding, and in a huff, took himself off into next door's garden.

As the days went by, the babies grew and I knew it wouldn't be long before they left their home. Coming home after work, I thought it was the mother bird sitting on my garden fence. But on a closer inspection, I saw it was one of her precious babies. Unfazed by the outside world, unafraid of me, he looked in my direction and cheeped. I couldn't help saying, 'What are you doing out little man?' I rushed inside for my camera, and took snap after snap, I'd only got a few chances. He looked at me and cheeped again. I wanted to stroke him. He was so tiny I was afraid he wouldn't last long with so many enemies about. I couldn't help myself as I offered up an extended finger. He immediately hopped on and clung tightly with black matchstick legs, his tiny claws needle sharp. He looked up at my face. Hopefully. He was hungry. My eyes filled with tears. For a few brief seconds I was held in a magical moment when a wild creature completely trusted me.

A couple of fluffy baby feathers detached themselves

from his soft plumage and drifted away, like thistledown, on the breeze. He picked at my fingernail. I put my camera down and gently stroked the soft blue head and primrose yellow chest. He appeared to enjoy this and his claws prickled as he tried to settle down and make himself more comfortable in my hand. Then there was a whirr of wings and mum was on the fence with a grub. When she saw that I was touching one of her babies, she flicked her tail from side to side, a sure sign of annoyance. She scolded, and the chick crouched, bewildered. The spell was broken, the precious moment over. I put him back in the box with his siblings, and in the morning they've all flown. Comforted with the thought that I had managed to get some pictures of this special moment, I was cruelly disappointed to find that the camera had a fault and every photo had been lost.

With three hundred letters, articles and photographs of mine being published over three years, earning me some street cred in writing, the late Steve Benz, of S.B.Publications asked if I could put together a book on Sussex crafts and industries special to the county. With computers still in their infancy, I became a regular visitor to the local libraries and set up live interviews, gathering useful, interesting information on local producers, such as trug basket and cricket bat makers. I wrote in-depth chapters on the iron, glass and pottery industry as well as the little known businesses such as needle makers and smockers.

One year and twenty – four chapters later and the book was finished.

A few days before the New Millennium there was a knock on the door. There stood Steve, holding a cardboard box.

"Here you are," he said, "I knew you would like to have your book out in time to celebrate 2000."

He handed me the parcel. I opened it. Inside were

a pile of paperbacks with sepia covers. In the centre, between a border of photographs, were the words,

"Made in Sussex"
Sussex crafts and Industries Past and Present.
Elizabeth Wright.

Holding a copy in my hands, I thought, 'Life can be very strange. This special moment would never have happened if it hadn't been for the discovery of that pair of fancy pants.'

WRITING BIOGRAPHY OF

ELIZABETH WRIGHT

I have been writing for a hobby for about fifty years; my first commercial successes were regular articles to "Cage and Aviary Birds" and "Birdkeeper" magazines. Spurred on by these acceptances, I then sold a feature on the famous Belle Tout lighthouse to "Sussex Life" and, rewriting the information, had that bought by "The Lady."

I decided to professionalise my work and did a distance college course with "Writers' Bureau." Having learnt much more about being a 'proper' writer, I managed to market over 300 features, fillers and letters during the next 3 years. These are some of the magazines they went to - "The Countryman," "Downs Today," "Parrots," "My Weekly," "Yours," "Best Of British," "Peoples' Friend," "Smallholder," "All about Cats," "Aspect County," "Tea," "Writers' News," "Dogs Today," "Taste," "Your Cat," "Comedy Connections," and many more. "Australian Bird Keeper" took a number of illustrated articles, as did USA's "Bird Times," and "American Cage Bird" magazine. Amusing pictures or funny jottings of mine have appeared many times in the Daily Mail's "Peterborough" columns.

Popular e-magazine, "Giddy Limits" uses a continuing supply of various features from me, which can be viewed on their excellent website. I also provide regular articles for the regional "Aspect County" magazine, under their "Working Wealden" section.

I am constantly looking for new markets where I can sell my work, and initial responses to my query letters appear to show that 2013 will be opening a few more doors.

I have been a long standing member of Eastbourne's highly successful "Anderida Writers," and a past winner of their coveted "Anderida Accolade."

Illustrations added to an article can often command payments equal to the value of the text. Although not a professional photographer, I have managed to sell a number of 'stand-alone' pictures to "Take a Break," "Pick me Up" and "Eastbourne Local Historian." One snap of a beach rescue was published on the front page of the "Eastbourne Herald." I have been just short of short listing in "Amateur Photographer" magazine's Photographers of the Year Competition, and was 2nd prize winner out of 18 in the Kingsmere Association's Photo competition. Meridian TV have used my shots of Belle Tout lighthouse at sunset and bluebells in Beaton's Wood, Arlington, as backdrops to the weather forecasters. East Sussex County Council chose my submission of a seated couple watching the sunset at Beachy Head to illustrate their informative book, "Forward at Fifty."

E-Articles credited to me can be found on www.TimeTravel-Britain.com.
www.waymark.com.

My first commissioned book was "Made in Sussex," (S.B. Publications.)
This covers 23 crafts and industries special to the county. Although now out of print, second-hand copies can be obtained through Amazon book

Publisher Phillimore's – The History Press, asked me to write a definitive work on the famous local Belle

Tout lighthouse. This will be available from all good bookshops and on line from the Amazon, Guardian and Telegraph websites I have added some humorous poetry to my repertoire, although, at present, much of this is just for fun.

In October 2011, I was invited by BBC Radio Sussex/ Surrey to take part in a live interview talking about my writing, my books and my life. An invitation for a return session is on offer.

I am now working on a sequel to "Fancy Pants", working title "Two up, one down," which is a hilarious account of the time my daughter and her then boyfriend, now partner, both lived with me. There were both social and cultural differences, plus an age gap. I was house proud pensioner, they were typical teenagers........

Visit my website....www.elizabethwright-thewriter.com

QUOTES

Liz Wright's book "From Fancy Pants to Getting There" is a cracking good read – full of humour, irony and pathos.

This true story of how she coped after the loss of both her cheating partner (through finding the fancy pants) and her business, shows what a gutsy, courageous woman she is – and a wonderful writer as well!

Tony Flood : Chairperson of Eastbourne's Anderida Writers and author of "The Secret Potion" and "My Life with the Stars."

Elizabeth brings her story so much to life that it's sitting, watching a hilarious, and at times, poignant play. Best read I've had for years.

Pam Rollison. "Down Your Way" – Eastbourne Herald.

This is one to keep. I laughed and cried all the way through. I hope we see much more of Ms Wright in the future.

Writer - Lindsay Crawford Jones

Elizabeth Wright's indomitable spirit and vibrant sense of humour shines through this pacey story of determination not to let the slings and arrows of life grind her down. It is also a tale that some of us can relate to only too well.

Jenny Jewiss – Writer and Vice-Chairperson of Eastbourne's Anderida Writers.

Lightning Source UK Ltd.
Milton Keynes UK
UKOW030832080513

210358UK00001B/10/P